1870 1871 1872 1873 1874 1875 1876 1877 1878 1879 1880 1881 1882 1883

- **1872** — H. Martyn Hart visits Denver
- **1874** — P. Voorhees Finch rector
- **1878** — H. Martyn Hart rector and dean
- **1880** — Cornerstone of first cathedral; first service in first cathedral
- **1872** — Bishop John Franklin Spalding
- **1876** — Emmanuel Church
- **1880** — Bishop and Chapter created
- **1874** — Trinity Memorial Chapel
- **1870** — Railroad reaches Denver, Denver census = 4,759
- **1873** — Panic of 1873
- **1876** — Colorado admitted to the Union, Battle of *The Little Big Horn*
- **1880** — Denver census = 35,629

1896 1897 1898 1899 1900 1901 1902 1903 1904 1905 1906 1907 1908 1909

- **1900** — Membership = 800
- **1902** — Cathedral burns, contest for new cathedral
- **1904** — Chapter house built; Schleier bells installed
- **1908** — Cornerstone of second cathedral
- **1902** — Bishop Charles S. Olmsted
- **1900** — Denver census = 133,859
- **1902** — First manned flight

1922 1923 1924 1925 1926 1927 1928 1929 1930 1931 1932 1933 1934 1935

- **1922** — Duncan Browne ...ship = 750
- **1924** — Benjamin Dagwell is dean, Canon Watts arrives, cathedral is consecrated
- **1926** — Parish house built
- **1930** — Membership = 1,144
- **1934** — Third clerestory window
- **1924** — St. Michael & All Angels Church
- **1926** — Bishop moves to St. John's
- **1930** — General Convention held in Denver
- **1922** — Woman suffrage amendment
- **1926** — Lindbergh Atlantic flight
- **1928** — Stock market crash
- **1930** — Great depression begins, Denver census = 287,861
- **1933** — Franklin D. Roosevelt elected

Saint John's Church in the Wilderness

A History of St. John's Cathedral in Denver, Colorado, 1860–2000

ROBERT IRVING WOODWARD

For
Gwen McGee
Best wishes
to a faithful member
of St. John's!

Woody
Robert I. Woodward
December 2001

To Nancy, my wife and best friend

Library of Congress Cataloging-in-Publication Data

Woodward, Robert Irving.
    Saint John's Church in the Wilderness: a history of St. John's Cathedral in Denver,
  Colorado. 1860-2000 / Robert Irving Woodward.
        p. cm.
    Includes bibliographic references and index.
    ISBN 0-938075-82-9
    I. St. John's Episcopal Cathedral (Denver, Colo.)--History. 2. Denver (Colo.)--Church
  history. I Title.

BX5980.D43 S849 2001
283'.78883-dc21   2001052043

Prairie Publishers, Inc.
390 Saint Paul Street
Denver, Colorado 80206

Cover photograph by Bill Baker, Cathedral Communications, with permission.

Printed in the United States of America.

05   04   03   02   01   1   2   3   4   5

First edition.

Contents

———⇒➤◦◄⇐———

Foreword

———✥———

DEAR READER, YOU HAVE IN YOUR HANDS a little jewel of a book, the life story of a great institution, told through the activities and creation of a multitude of people over a period of one hundred and forty years. I use the word "little" advisedly, for without selection of people and events, a thorough history of St. John's would have enlarged to several weighty volumes.

As it is, the size is just right, the choice of relevant activities leading you to a greater understanding of all the issues involved at moments of change. As a lifelong member of the congregation, as choir boy, acolyte, and teacher, I deeply appreciate the care with which this narrative was constructed. The pictures are just right, the use of quotations carefully acknowledged. And the whole work invokes memories. I can remember as a very young boy listening to Dean Hart give a sermon involving the parable of the mustard seed; later, Sunday School classes in the old chapter house, playing ball on the sandlot where Dagwell Hall now sits.

The evolution of the liturgy is shown in the pictures. One wonders what Dean Hart would say of the whole liturgical movement of our time. My earliest memory is that of Dean Dagwell using eucharistic vestments in services at St. Martin's Chapel: they were white, without ornamentation. From that, it was an easy step to the use of an elaborate set of vestments, used only on major festivals, and then on to vestments for celebrant, deacon, and subdeacon at cathedral services. All this was made possible by the liturgical reform movement that produced the 1979 Prayer Book and accompanying rules that made the Eucharist the common service at all times.

The long association of Bob and Nancy Woodward with the cathedral (as the text shows, she is a fourth-generation member) and their longtime services as cathedral archivists have brought to this work a completeness which deserves high praise.

Allen duPont Breck
August 24, 2000

Allen duPont Breck, Ph.D.
August 21, 1914–October 11, 2000
Historiographer of the Diocese of
Colorado, Professor Emeritus of
History, The University of Denver.

Preface

———⟫•⟪———

SAINT JOHN'S CHURCH IN THE WILDERNESS: Is that really the name of the impressive Gothic cathedral that stands on 14th Avenue between Washington and Clarkson streets? Well, yes—and no. The name of the cathedral is just one of the many fascinating things that the study of the history of St. John's reveals. The story of the church is the story of the many people, clergy and laity, that joined together to worship the Lord in this place. It parallels the story of Denver from the beginnings of both in 1860 in a remote wilderness in the West to the year 2000 in a complex city that is no less a wilderness.

The church organized one hundred and forty years ago was first referred to as the Church of Saint John's in the Wilderness, the name of the organization even before there was a church building. Years later it was said that the name had referred to the fact that the nearest Episcopal church was seven hundred miles away in Kansas. The ladies of the church held an Evening Festival for the

Church on June 24, 1861, St. John the Baptist day, which suggests that the church might have been named for St. John the Baptist. In September of the same year at the first session of the Legislative Assembly of the Territory of Colorado, the church was "hereby incorporated as a religious society, under the corporate style of Saint John's Church in the Wilderness." Later, when the congregation moved into its first building, it was also called Saint John's Church in the Wilderness. Bishop Johnson reported some sixty-three years later that when the little church building was consecrated in 1862, it was solemnly dedicated to the memory of St. John the Baptist. Newspapers of the period verify that the little church building was called Saint John's Church in the Wilderness.

Then enters Bishop Spalding, who in 1880 enacted canon XXI, which said that "The Church of Saint John the Evangelist, Denver, is hereby adopted, and constituted the Cathedral Church of the Jurisdiction of Colorado." He then incorporated the Bishop and Chapter and said that the rector of St. John's "shall take rank next after the Bishop, and shall bear the title of The Very Reverend, the Dean of the Cathedral of St. John the Evangelist." The first cathedral building was referred to by the bishop as the Cathedral of Saint John the Evangelist; however, Dean Hart referred to it only as St. John's Cathedral. By the time the second cathedral was built, even Dean Hart had embraced the "Evangelist" title. The architectural drawings and the laying of the foundation stone were for the Cathedral of Saint John the Evangelist. The symbolism found in the carved stone at the main entrance, the brass eagle lectern, and the figure in the window over the altar are all of St. John the Evangelist.

Now in the year 2000 the congregation (corporation) is still Saint John's Church in the Wilderness, and the present building is really the Cathedral of Saint John the Evangelist. However, you can call the cathedral anything you want, but I think that Dean Hart had it right in 1880—it's just St. John's Cathedral.

Robert I. Woodward

Acknowledgments

———⟶•0•⟵———

IN THE SPRING OF 1985, I ENROLLED IN A DENVER history class at the University of Colorado at the urging of Tom Noel, then an assistant professor of history at the Denver campus. My assignment in Tom's class was to write something about St. John's. It's taken me fifteen years, but I've finally done it!

Beginning in 1988, I wrote a series of historical articles for *The Open Door*, and in 1995 my wife Nancy and I taught a five-week St. John's History class as a part of the cathedral Adult Forum on Sunday mornings. My students suggested that I should use the lesson plans of these classes as the beginnings of this book.

None of this would have been possible without the encouragement and participation of my wife, Nancy. As co-archivists of St. John's since 1985, we have a partnership that has allowed us both to enjoy and learn so much about this church. She has kept me on the track when I have veered away. Nancy is a fourth-generation member of St. John's and has attended under six of the eight deans of the cathedral. We are both fourth-generation Denverites and live in an 1890 home that is a Denver Landmark and a frequent meeting place for members of the cathedral parish.

Most of the research for this book has been done in the cathedral archives. It is to the credit of Louisa Arps, the first archivist; the Women of St. John's, who provided the initial funding for the archives; and to Dean Herbert Barrall, who together created the first formal archives for Saint John's Church in the Wilderness. Louisa collected material from all over the cathedral complex and organized it so that it can be utilized. The Women of St. John's funded the construction of the vault in the Roberts Building, and Dean Barrall was the leader who made it all possible. We are especially grateful to have had the opportunity to work with Louisa Arps for the year preceding her death.

We offer our thanks to Dean Donald McPhail who had enough faith in us to appoint us archivists, and to make it possible for us to learn how to be archivists through the course "Beyond the Basics," at the Friars of the Atonement Archives at Graymoor, Garrison, New York; and to Dean Charles Kiblinger, who has allowed us to continue in this position. That the book is in the proper form, I thank Jeanne Collins, my editor, who has been incredibly patient with my untrained writing. Jeanne also interviewed the clergy for the last chapter: "The Kiblinger Years."

Most of the photographs are from the wonderful collection in the archives. Many of them are loaned by the Denver Public Library Western History Department and the Colorado Historical Society. Others are from church members and professional photographers, some identified and some not, which have been given to the parish over a period of many years.

It's been a long time coming, but it has been a rewarding experience.

1. The Church in the Wilderness, 1860–1879

WHAT WAS THIS PLACE WE NOW CALL DENVER really like before it was Denver? Before 1858 the area was inhabited only by Cheyennes, Arapahoes, and Utes, and a few white trappers. In 1858 the trappers found small amounts of gold where Cherry Creek meets the Platte River, an event that would forever change the face of the Rocky Mountains and the Great American Desert. When word of gold reached "the States," hundreds of fortune seekers set out for the Pike's Peak gold region in Kansas Territory.

By 1859 a settlement of tents and log cabins called Auraria huddled on the west side of Cherry Creek; on the east side was a similar settlement called St. Charles, but soon renamed Denver, with the two camps numbering about fifteen hundred people. There were a few businesses (mainly saloons and gambling halls), muddy streets, no trees, and little law and order. The two towns were combined in the spring of 1860 as Denver City, but Denver would not become a legal municipality until November 1861, when Congress recognized Colorado Territory.

Among those who came to make their fortunes in the gold fields were town builders; and among the town builders were two men who would play a pivotal role in the establishment of an Episcopal church. One was Jack Kehler, appointed sheriff of Arapahoe County, Kansas Territory, who spent much of his time at his mining claim at Mountain City, a now-unknown spot between the present towns of Central City and Blackhawk. The second was Thomas Bayaud, a merchant and builder who read "Episcopal services" at the confluence of Cherry Creek and the Platte River.

Meanwhile, back in the States, the approaching Civil War was deeply affecting the lives of those who lived along the Potomac River in northern Virginia and Maryland. The Reverend John Kehler, Jack's father, was in charge of a small Episcopal church at Sharpsburg, Maryland, only twelve miles from Charles Town, Virginia, where John Brown was hanged on December 2, 1859, after having seized the arsenal at Harper's Ferry. Kehler had served twenty-one years as a Lutheran minister and in 1840 had been the pastor of a large Evangelical Lutheran church in Cumberland, Maryland, when he applied to become an Episcopal priest. Bishop William Whittingham of Maryland promptly accepted him. For another eighteen years he served on both sides of the Potomac at such places as Shepardstown and Harper's Ferry in Virginia (now West Virginia) and Hagerstown, Antietam, Boonsboro, Harmony Hill, and finally Sharpsburg, all in Maryland.

The little mission church in Sharpsburg was not exactly a success as Kehler's Union leanings made him less than popular along the Potomac. On October 1, 1859, his wife died at the age of fifty-seven. Soon after, he received a

Thomas J. Bayaud, lumber merchant and builder who read "Episcopal services" in Denver before there was an Episcopal church, and the first senior warden of Saint John's Church in the Wilderness. He died at Sterling City, north of Fairplay, in January 1865. *Courtesy, Colorado Historical Society, F5234.*

St. Paul's Episcopal Church, Father Kehler's parish in Sharpsburg, Maryland, which was rebuilt following the Civil War. *Photo by Robert C. Black, III, 1987.*

letter from his son Jack, the sheriff of Arapahoe County, urging him to come to Kansas Territory. We do not know whether the Reverend Kehler was aware of how bad the conditions were in Denver, but in mid-December he wrote to Bishop Whittingham:

> In compliance with the earnest entreaties of my son, who is now in Kansas [Territory], and trusting that I may prove useful in the church—I have made up my mind to remove thither. . . . There is a great opening in Kansas for ministers of the church, I learn. The Bishop will please give me letter dimissory from the Diocese of Maryland to that of Kansas.[1]

However, Denver was not a part of the diocese of Kansas, so there was really no jurisdiction to which Kehler could technically transfer.

Nevertheless, two days after Christmas in 1859, the Kehlers left Sharpsburg. The party consisted of daughters, Crimora (23), Bettie (21), and Mollie (20); a son Willie (17), named for Bishop Whittingham; and a grand-daughter Nannie Clarke (11), the daughter of Kehler's daughter Pigeon who lived in Washington, D.C. Kehler himself turned sixty-three during the trip. They reached Leavenworth, Kansas Territory, only four days later. On January 11, 1860, the *Leavenworth Daily Times* reported:

> The Pike's Peak express left yesterday for Denver with six passengers, Mr. Keiler [sic], three daughters, all young ladies, one son and a granddaughter. We venture the assertion that the Express never took a more valuable cargo, and the bachelors of the diggings will coincide with us! Mr. Keiler [sic] goes out to establish an Episcopal Church.

The Kehlers arrived in Denver seven days later. Jack ushered them from the stage to the two-story brick house that he had built for them at 18th and Larimer

The Reverend John H. Kehler. From a tintype probably taken just before or soon after his coming to Denver in January 1860. *Cathedral archives.*

streets. It was the only brick building in Denver except for the powder magazine.[2]

The next day John Kehler distributed handbills announcing a meeting to be held January 24 to organize an Episcopal church. The *Rocky Mountain News* reported this meeting the next day, quoting Reverend Kehler:

> The object of this meeting has been learned from the cards that have been circulated. In those cards an invitation has been extended to Episcopalians, and all other citizens friendly to the creation of an Episcopalian Church in the City of Denver—to assemble for the purpose of taking steps preparatory to the accomplishment of the object alluded to.[3]

On January 29, 1860, the first service was held in a dirt-floored log cabin called the Union School House, almost in the bed of Cherry Creek at 14th and McGaa [now Market] streets. Of this service, Father Kehler wrote in his diary:

> Doubtless, since the creation, this was the first time that the sublime and befitting sentence was uttered in this remote region and in full view of the far famed "Rocky Mountains," "The Lord is in His holy temple, let all the earth keep silence before Him." The collection on the occasion amounted to $8.85.[4]

A temporary vestry elected on February 19 included Thomas Bayaud, senior warden; Samuel Curtis, junior warden; Charles Lawrence (all of whom have streets named for them); and Amos Steck, soon to become mayor of Denver. It also included a young man named Thomas Wildman, who wrote his mother and sister in Danbury, Connecticut, on February 22, 1860:

> Now then I will give you some of the Religious intelligence of our city. The Rev. Mr. Kehler and three daughters arrived from Virginia

[actually Maryland] about six weeks ago and we have had preaching once a day at 10 o'clock for four Sundays. Last Sunday after service the male members of the congregation were invited to attend—or rather remain—after service, which placed me in rather an unpleasant situation, as I had accompanied one of the daughters to Church; but I finally concluded that she would excuse me if I should obey the request of her father. We had an election of Vestrymen to act until Easter Monday, which, according to the canons of the Church, is the day for the election of officers. Your son was elected one of the vestrymen and felt highly complimented not only by the office but because the one who proposed his name happened to be our Pastor.[5]

Thomas Wildman's letter continues: "We the vestrymen, are going ahead now being bound that an Episcopal Church shall be the first one at the foot of the Rocky Mountains.[6] We have given it a very appropriate name: It is being called the Church of St. John in the Wilderness."[7] The story has it that the name for St. John's was suggested by a young man named William Moore, because the closest Episcopal church was in Kansas, seven hundred miles away.[8]

Father Kehler's daughter must have excused the young vestryman for his delay in escorting her home, for in September, Mollie Kehler married Thomas Wildman, and at the same time Crimora Kehler married Henry Rogers. The double wedding at the rectory was *the* social event of the season. The social event of the Christmas season was St. John's Festival, perhaps the first bazaar, on December 20.

Because of his white hair, which he wore long over his collar, the elderly clergyman immediately and affectionately became known as Father Kehler in this country of young adventurers. Services were held at several locations during the first two years, including the Apollo Theatre above a gambling hall on Larimer Street and the Thomas Bayaud business rooms above a wholesale liquor store. The first communion service was held at Christmas, 1860, when seven

North side of Larimer Street between 14th and 15th streets, 1861. St. John's held services upstairs in Apollo Hall (second building from left). *Photo by W. G. Chamberlain. Courtesy, Denver Public Library, Western History Department, F10268.*

Thomas G. Wildman, vestryman and Kehler's son-in-law. His letters to his family in Connecticut tell much about the beginnings of Saint John's Church in the Wilderness. *Courtesy, Colorado Historical Society, F20484.*

Bishop Joseph Cruikshank
Talbot, the "Bishop of
all outdoors," early 1860s.
*Courtesy, Colorado Historical
Society, F5190.*

persons received communion. Jack, the sheriff, frequently deputized his father to attend murderers to the gallows and to bury them and their victims in Prospect Hill Cemetery [present Cheeseman Park]. Father Kehler would eventually bury both of his sons there as well.

On February 15, 1860, Denver became part of the newly created missionary district of the North-West, which included Montana, Wyoming, the Dakotas, Nebraska, Colorado, Utah, and Nevada; the bishop was Joseph Cruikshank Talbot, who called himself "the bishop of all outdoors." On his first visit to Denver in August 1861, he was amazed to find the church already established.

In his first report to the Board of Missions, Bishop Talbot states:

August 5, Monday. I resumed my seat in the coach at Julesburg and arrived in Denver at 3 am on Wednesday following. Here I was kindly

welcomed and hospitably entertained by the rector, Rev. Mr. Kehler.
. . . The labors of The Rev. Mr. Kehler in this place have been blessed.
I found a large room, comfortably fitted up with chancel, desk, pulpit,
etc., and quite filled by a congregation of intelligent and apparently
earnest worshippers.[9]

On November 6, 1861, at the first session of the Legislative Assembly of
the new Territory of Colorado, the little congregation was incorporated as a religious society, "under the corporate style of Saint John's Church in the Wilderness," which remains the official name of the parish.

Father Kehler had escaped the conflict in the South, but he could not
escape the Civil War entirely. Kehler was appointed chaplain of the First Regiment of the Colorado Volunteers in November 1861, after John Chivington, a
Methodist minister, had refused the appointment and taken a command position.[10] For several months Kehler conducted weekly services at Camp Weld, located at what is now the west end of the Eighth Avenue viaduct. At the battle
of Glorieta Pass, near Santa Fe, New Mexico, on March 26, 1862, Colonel
Chivington and the Colorado Volunteers "saved the West" for the Union. This
was the only Civil War battle in the West. Chaplain Kehler was ordered to New
Mexico in June 1862 and submitted his resignation to the vestry of St. John's.
Before he left, he married his daughter Bettie to Major John S. Fillmore, pay-
master of the Colorado Volunteers. The next day, he and Major Fillmore left for
Fort Craig, New Mexico.

Two years earlier, in August 1860, the Methodist Church South had built
a small brick church at 14th and Arapahoe streets, now the site of the Executive
Tower Inn. This was the first church building in Denver and was abandoned by
the Southern Methodists when the Civil War began. Through the arrangements
of the newly elected senior warden, Chief Justice Benjamin Franklin Hall, the
vestry of St. John's purchased this building. The new church building was dedicated by Bishop Talbot on July 20, 1862. This little building was twice enlarged,

Saint John's Church in the Wilderness at 14th and Arapahoe streets, after the first enlargement in 1862. *Courtesy, Colorado Historical Society, F3898.*

and served Saint John's Church in the Wilderness for eighteen years. Soon after acquiring the building, the congregation had an interim rector, Isaac Hagar, deacon, who was missionary-at-large for Bishop Talbot in Nebraska. He remained only five months. In December 1862, the vestry voted that, in addition to paying the Reverend Hagar's salary of $100 per month, his coach fare to the Missouri River would be paid.

     With the assistance of Bishop Talbot, a new rector had already been called, the Reverend Horace Baldwin Hitchings of Connecticut. Dr. Allen Breck, in *The Episcopal Church in Colorado*, colorfully explains:

> The Rev. Mr. Hitchings in his quiet country parish in Connecticut was greatly astonished to receive a call as rector to a parish in Denver.

The Reverend
Isaac Hagar,
deacon and
acting rector in
1862. *Courtesy,
Colorado
Episcopalian.*

The Reverend
Horace Baldwin
Hitchings, second
rector of Saint
John's Church in
the Wilderness,
1862–1869. *Courtesy,
Colorado Historical
Society, F3242.*

He had never heard of Denver or Colorado, and a most diligent search in the latest and most authentic maps gave no information as to the locality of the town. He concluded some college friends had been playing a joke on him, and put the call aside, giving no serious thought, until a letter came from Bishop Talbot. . . . Denver was reality and the call was genuine.[11]

Hitchings began his service in December 1862, but was not installed as rector until Bishop Talbot again came to Denver in August 1863. While in Denver he began to accumulate what would eventually be a sizeable fortune by buying claims and properties from those who found themselves unsuited to the life in the wilderness and wished to go back home. The land he bought was worthless at the time but eventually became valuable as Denver grew. He served as rector of Saint John's Church in the Wilderness for seven years: through the Denver fire of 1863, the Cherry Creek flood of 1864, and the Indian wars of 1864–1869. During this time Father Kehler returned to Denver and occasionally assisted the young rector.[12] The Reverend Hitchings left Denver in 1869.[13]

Going back a few years, to 1866, Right Reverend George M. Randall had replaced Bishop Talbot as missionary bishop of Colorado, which now included only Colorado, Wyoming, Idaho, Montana, and later New Mexico. Following the Reverend Hitchings' departure from Denver in 1869, the vestry of St. John's asked Bishop Randall to become rector. He served as both bishop and rector until his death. When it was suggested that he have help in his ministry he said he would "rather wear out than rust out," and he did! His last service was at the Shoshone agency in Wyoming in August 1873, where he baptized three of Sacajawea's[14] great-grandchildren. Bishop Randall died in September of 1873.

The Reverend Walter H. Moore,[15] who had been serving Grace Church in Georgetown, Colorado, was asked by the vestry to act as rector of the parish from October 1 until Easter of 1874. During this time the St. John's Sunday School had opened a mission school near 26th and Curtis streets, a location

"Father" Kehler's portrait by W. G. Chamberlain reflects the hard times in the frontier town of Denver in the mid-1860s. *Courtesy, Denver Public Library, Western History Collection.*

Horace Hitchings returned to Denver from New York following his retirement and served as rector emeritus 1910–1917. *Cathedral archives.*

The Right
Reverend George
M. Randall,
missionary bishop
of Colorado and
Parts Adjacent, and
rector of Saint
John's Church in
the Wilderness,
1869–1873. *Courtesy,
Denver Public Library,
Western History
Collection.*

The Reverend
Peter Voorhees
Finch, rector,
1874–1878. This
photo was taken
a few years later at
St. James' Church,
Greenfield,
Massachusetts.
Cathedral archives.

Emmanuel Episcopal Church, built in 1876, and the site of the Cathedral's St. Andrew's Mission, 1892–1902. *Courtesy, Colorado Historical Society, F2128.*

some distance out of town. The new bishop, John Franklin Spalding, laid the cornerstone for the second Episcopal church building in Denver, Trinity Memorial Chapel, in memory of Bishop Randall, on March 18. The bishop named the Reverend Moore as its first rector. Moore did not stay at Trinity Memorial for long; he soon left Colorado for Illinois where he later became dean of St. John's Cathedral in Quincy.

Following his consecration but before he came to Colorado, Bishop Spalding had recommended the Reverend P. Voorhees Finch of Pittsburgh to be rector. The bishop wrote, "I am so clear in the opinion that he is the man we need that I respectfully urge you to give him at once a positive and strong call. . . . He is a rare man and you will be most fortunate to secure him."[16] Finch

Emmanuel Sherith Israel Chapel/Student Art Gallery, still standing on the Auraria campus. The roof line was modified by the Jewish congregation that purchased this building in 1903. *Photo by James Milmoe. Courtesy, Colorado Historical Society, F11302.*

accepted the call to be rector in February 1874. Among the accomplishments during his time of service was another new Episcopal church in Denver. At this time, Thomas Clayton, the superintendent of St. John's Sunday School, who had helped start Trinity Memorial in East Denver, turned his attention to West Denver. The new mission Sunday School soon had ninety children, and the bishop's wife was included among the teachers. In 1876, Bishop Spalding conse-crated Emmanuel Church, which was built at 10th and Lawrence streets. The Emmanuel congregation built a new church in 1892 and, for about ten years, the St. Andrew's Society of the Cathedral conducted services in the old building, which was then called the St. Andrew's Mission. The building was sold to a Jew-ish congregation in 1903.[17]

For several years Finch tried to raise money to build a new church for St. John's, but without success. At a vestry meeting on October 7, 1878, it was re-solved that "it is not expedient at this time to undertake the building of a new

Saint John's Church at 14th and Arapahoe after the second enlargement, about 1870. "The first iron bell in Denver" hangs in the windmill-like tower. *Courtesy, Denver Public Library, Western History Department, F11588.*

Interior of Saint John's Church, ca. 1870. "The ceiling was of sagging canvas." *Courtesy, Denver Public Library, Western History Department.*

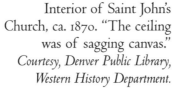

church." Following the resolution, P. Voorhees Finch's letter of resignation, to take effect at Easter, was read. Saint John's Church in the Wilderness was again looking for a new rector.

The beginnings
of St. John's,
1860–1862

The Episcopal
Church grows,
1874–1880

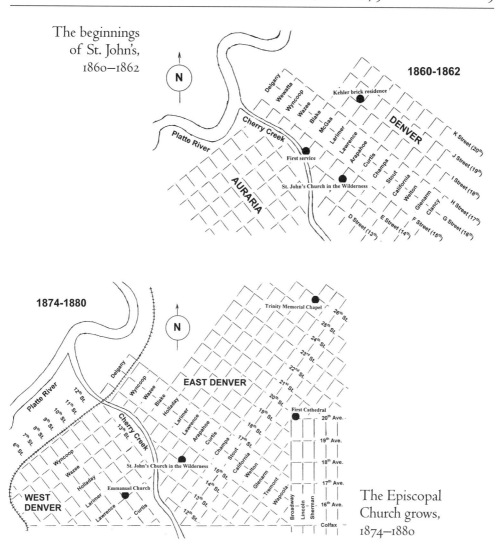

2. *The Great Dean and the First Cathedral, 1879–1903*

THE VESTRY CALLED THE REVEREND H. MARTYN HART to be rector of St. John's on March 12, 1879. How did a young cleric from suburban London become the first-choice candidate for a church in the western frontier of America?

Hart was born on March 3, 1838, the son of an English vicar at Otley, near York in northern England. He grew up exposed to the disciplined work habits of education administered by a young Scottish schoolmaster imported to educate the young men of the town.[18] He studied science, mathematics, and medicine, graduating from Trinity College, Dublin in 1861 and became a mathematical assistant at the Blackheath Preparatory School in that London suburb. He soon married the sister of the headmaster and took his post at the school when his brother-in-law took a position at King's College, London. Even though he had no formal theological education, after some eight or nine years he was ordained by the archbishop of Canterbury and became the rector of St. German's Church in Blackheath in 1871. Hart describes his work schedule:

> School, honestly teaching all day till five o'clock; Church, two sermons every Sunday to a congregation largely composed of successful London merchants and professional men; public meetings almost every night to direct committees to organize their charities; and writing considerably . . . Geological, Mineralogical and Chemical Articles for *Popular Educator.*[19]

He lost weight and sleep and finally suffered what he called a hemorrhage. By the fall of 1872 he needed a rest and a change of climate. At the same time a parishioner was looking for someone to sail around the world with his son, who needed to spend some time with a decent companion. Leaving his wife and children, Hart and the young man set sail for America.

After spending time in New York City, Niagara, and Chicago, the two men took the train to Kansas Territory to hunt buffalo. After satisfying their urge to hunt,[20] they asked where else the train went and were told it went to a town called Denver. On arriving in Denver, they stayed at the Delmonico of the West, "the only hostel in Denver which was fit for two such eminent people," according to the train conductor.[21] The Reverend Hart preached two Sundays at the little brick and wood church called Saint John's Church in the Wilderness at 14th and Arapahoe streets. He also gave a lecture on the zoology of the sea.[22] The pair traveled on to Salt Lake City, San Francisco, and then across the Pacific to Japan, China, and India. They returned to Blackheath, England, in the spring of 1873, some six months after they had left.

The Reverend Hart must have made a good impression on the little church in Denver because the vestry contacted him in 1873 following Bishop

H. Martyn Hart, the
young student from
Otley, England, ca.
1855. *Cathedral archives.*

Hart's home,
one wing of
the Blackheath
Preparatory
School near
London. *Photo
by William Lea,
1959. Cathedral
archives.*

Randall's death, but he was not interested in coming to Denver at that time. Five years later, in 1878, the vestry of St. John's again wrote to Hart in Blackheath to see if he would be interested in a call to Denver. Hart later quoted from this "letter from my dear friend, Mr. Charles D. Cobb" (secretary of the vestry):

> On this side of the Atlantic all the indications of Providence point toward you and seem to favor your coming. You, an entire stranger and foreigner, visiting us briefly, have been held in almost affectionate memory for six or seven years, and your name is first upon the lips of all those who then met or heard you, whenever the question of a Rector comes up. We knew not whether you were living or dead, married or single, "High" or "Low," famous or obscure, but the feeling was unanimous and almost an ardent longing.[23]

The vestry also wrote to the bishop of London who forwarded the letter to the bishop of Rochester. At a vestry meeting in January of 1879, a communication was read from the bishop, stating that:

> He had interviewed The Rev. Martyn Hart touching his willingness to cross the Atlantic . . . that while Mr. Hart was much gratified by the kindly recollection of him, he preferred to remain in his native country.[24]

Disappointed, the vestry proceeded to consider others, and a few days later extended a call to the Reverend John Houghton of Salem, Washington County, New York. Within days the vestry received a cablegram from Hart stating that he was interested in the position. The vestry was stunned. Their dilemma was soon resolved when the Reverend Houghton declined the call.[25]

The call for Hart to be rector was offered in a wonderful five-page letter from Charles Cobb, which described Denver and some of the changes since 1872:

Denver—now with a population of 25,000 is the capital and metropolis and will always be at least the latter and the center of wealth and refinement. As a city it is wonderfully improved since you were here. No longer in the midst of a barren plain—it is almost embowered in the shade of cultivated trees. We have streetcars, gas, and more recently the telephone. We are growing steadily and substantially. If there is to be any great interior city west of Chicago and St. Louis, there seems to be little doubt but that it will be Denver.[26]

He then compares the economic situation to England's, including the cost of flour, beef, milk, and butter, and discusses the bishop and the Episcopal schools. About St. John's he says:

We now have a boy choir and a pretty efficient organist, but there is occasion for improvement in the choir. Our parish, while lacking somewhat in vital, spiritual life, is not torn by dissension or partisanship. Our prevalent standard of churchmanship is inclined to be low or evangelical—perhaps a little too much so. I write from the standpoint of a moderate high-churchman.

He also mentioned the fact that there had been only nineteen days without sunshine since July of 1872, when Hart had last visited Denver.

In May the vestry cabled Hart five hundred dollars to "come out and get acquainted with the people of the parish," and Hart immediately set out. He hoped to find some reason not to leave London and move to Denver; but he found none except loss of income.[27]

Hart soon accepted the call to be rector of Saint John's Church in the Wilderness. He wrote about his arrival:

After a safe journey, eleven of us—six children, a governess, and two maids—arrived in Denver on a Saturday, which was Michaelmas

Day,[28] 1879; and we at once experienced the thoughtful kindness of our new American friends, for they had taken a furnished house for us, spread an ample dinner, and left us to ourselves.[29]

Hart later recalled the time when he had accepted the call:

> I do not wonder that when it came to my actual starting, the manager of the largest bank in London urged my dear friend and Churchwarden to go with him to a Master of Lunacy and get an order to lock me up in an asylum for six months until I came to my senses! But I was an officer in a big army and I became convinced that I had received orders to go to Denver and I was thankful that the order had not been to the centre of Africa.[30]

Bishop Spalding had already written to Hart about his hope of establishing a "cathedral system." He felt that this was the proper type of organization for his missionary district.[31] According to Hart, "The Bishop's plan sounded to me eminently sensible. It was indeed a return to the medieval system, when the Church was at the zenith of her power and usefulness. . . . I was to be the Dean."[32] Shortly after Hart's arrival in Denver, the bishop gave him a letter of appointment.[33] Hart assumed from this letter that St. John's was elevated to the status of cathedral and all the other parishes were, in a sense, reduced to the status of missions. The letter implied that as dean and principal cleric under the bishop, he was to have jurisdiction over all missionary activity and, therefore, over the other clergy. In April of 1880, the bishop took action to create the formal corporation known as "The Bishop and Chapter of the Cathedral of Saint John the Evangelist, Denver, Colorado."

At this point, based on his understanding of the cathedral system, Dean Hart attempted to carry out the duties of the "Dean of Denver." He soon came to realize that the other clergy resented the whole idea of a cathedral and would

H. Martyn Hart, the
fifth rector of Saint
John's Church in the
Wilderness and the
first dean of St. John's
Cathedral. *Cathedral
archives.*

John Franklin Spalding, missionary
bishop of Colorado and Wyoming,
with oversight of Arizona and
New Mexico, 1873–1887; and first
bishop of Colorado, 1887–1902.
He instituted the "cathedral
system" for the Colorado
missionary district. *Cathedral archives.*

not take any direction from him. It is probable that the bishop intended to have the cathedral as the center of work for his diocese; for his cathedral system was designed to have control over missions, educational activities, and coordination among parishes, with the rectors of the parishes as canons of the cathedral, helping in the total work of the diocese. But it is also probable that he had not worked out the pecking order that it required. When confronted with the dean's assumption of authority, the bishop denied that he had given Hart such power.

There is no doubt that both Hart and the bishop were stubborn and outspoken. Once embroiled in argument, it was hard for either man to back down and admit he might have been wrong. Neither was untruthful, but both tended to exaggerate. This was just the beginning of the troubles between Dean Hart and Bishop Spalding. As the years went by, there were misunderstandings, accusations, and bitter arguments between them, and the issues were many. At one point a "Council of Conciliation" made up of five bishops was appointed by the presiding bishop to mediate between them. As a result of their action, Dean Hart withdrew any "language of disparagement" that he might have used; and the bishop agreed to resume his Episcopal visitations to St. John's. It was a fragile peace.

The situation was also complicated by the fact that the vestry of St. John's was more concerned with the affairs of the parish church than with the cathedral system and resented the bishop's intrusion into their affairs. A deed had previously been granted to St. John's, which conveyed property from the bishop to St. John's vestry for use in building a new cathedral. Sensing that to carry out the bishop's concept of building a cathedral system was impossible, Hart turned his energies to erecting a much larger church (a cathedral) to house his own congregation. The bishop encouraged him.

The structure was designed by Messrs. Lloyd & Pearce of Detroit, who had built a church for Bishop Spalding when he was rector of a church in Erie, Pennsylvania. The plan was to build a brick "interior," which someday would be

The proposed new cathedral of St. John the Evangelist, to be located at 20th and Welton Streets (where Broadway terminated at that time). Sketch shows a tower that was never built. *Cathedral archives.*

covered with a red sandstone exterior.[34] The laying of the cornerstone on September 21, 1880, was a glorious affair. Seats were hired from a traveling circus. The Masons, Odd Fellows, Knights of Pythias, firemen, the artillery, the police, and "a strong array of Churchmen" were there. Dean Hart later reported:

> There must have been a crowd of ten thousand people. Bishop Spalding laid the stone, the Stars and Stripes went up, the band played, the choir and congregation sang, the canons roared and broke the windowpanes of the nearest cottages. There never was such enthusiasm, and Bishop Spalding was so elated that he made an address on Cathedral Systems for three-quarters of an hour.[35]

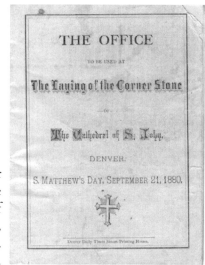

Service leaflet for
the laying of the
cornerstone of
the first cathedral,
September 21, 1880.
Cathedral archives.

Two years after Dean Hart's arrival, the last service was held on November 7, 1881, in the old church at 14th and Arapahoe streets and four hundred people processed up 14th Street to Welton Street to the opening service of the third Episcopal cathedral building built in the United States. This first cathedral in Denver was a Victorian Romanesque structure located at 20th and Welton streets, one block north of the later site of Trinity Methodist Church.[36] On the same site, called the Cathedral Close, were Matthews Hall, the theological school where the bishop lived; Jarvis Hall, a school for boys; a cottage for the principal; a gymnasium; and the deanery.

The dimensions of the building as reported in contemporary newspapers appear to be exaggerated, as was the reported seating capacity of the nave. A "plan of pews" found in Dean Hart's scrapbook indicates that the nave seated about 860 rather than the 1,200 reported, making the seating capacity about the same as the present nave before the removal of several ranks of pews. The chancel was sixty feet deep and accommodated a choir of sixty. To the south of

The first St. John's Cathedral, ca. 1885, at the intersection of Welton Street and Broadway (where Broadway ended). To the left of the cathedral is Welton going northeast and to the right is the very narrow 20th Avenue going east. The building behind the cathedral facing Welton is the deanery. *Courtesy, Colorado Historical Society, F13835.*

Easter, ca. 1885, the nave of the first cathedral. The rood screen reads "Alleluia, The Lord is Risen, Alleluia." Note the baptismal font, which is still in use. *Photo by J. Collier, Denver. Cathedral archives.*

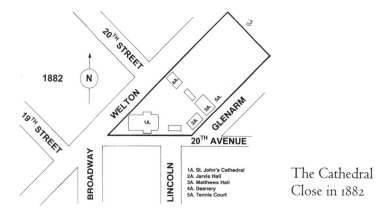

The Cathedral
Close in 1882

the chancel was the "lady choir," accommodating up to thirty women's voices, which augmented the men's and boys' choir and yet were not physically in the chancel. Under the chancel was the chapel, and under the nave was the crypt, which was used for Sunday School and meetings. The stained-glass windows were especially noteworthy; all but one were from the studio of Edward Frampton of London. The most spectacular window was a representation of the Crucifixion, for which the artist went to Antwerp and copied Van Dyck's *Christ*. This window was given in memory of Thomas Bayaud, the first senior warden of Saint John's Church in the Wilderness. The wrought iron and brass rood screen, now in the present cathedral, was added in 1888. The interior of the cathedral was redecorated, and the carved oak reredos from Oberammergau, also in the present cathedral, was added in 1902.

Dean Hart was a complex person—a crusader and a visionary who was controversial, flamboyant, dedicated, and compassionate. He waged a running battle with the press. One newspaper reported:

> The dean for a long time, year after year, actually insisted that he
> never read a Denver newspaper. They were so wicked, so unreli-

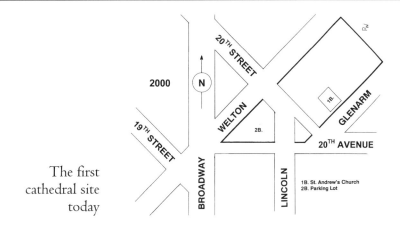

The first
cathedral site
today

able, so very unlike his favorite London paper of old, that he would
neither offend his mind nor soil his hands with them. He no doubt
repeated ten thousand times that he never, never defiled his eyes with
a Denver newspaper; and yet there was never a single line item in a
Denver paper reflecting either upon the Dean or St. John's Cathedral,
though they were tucked away in the paper's remotest corner, that
didn't call forth from the Dean a half column reply in the very next
issue.[37]

Sometimes the press had good things to say about the dean:

Yes, the newspapers all like the Dean. He is so eccentric in his notions
of morals, yet withal so good—so good at heart, so liberal with his
means, so untiring in relieving suffering, so busy, so brusque, so comi-
cal, so deucedly English in speech, so pathetic and often so funny that
he would be a strange creature, who, knowing him, didn't like him. He
is the Robin Hood of the ministry. Nothing delights him more than
to "hold up" a millionaire that he may empty his plunder into the lap
of some suffering waif.[38]

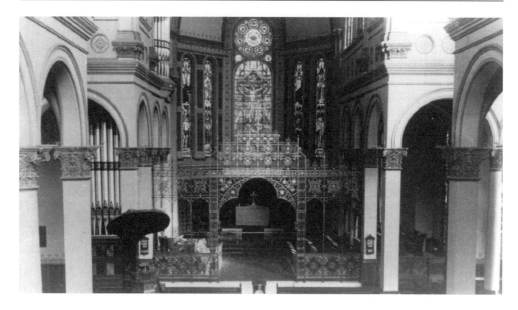

Chancel of the first cathedral at 20th and Welton Streets, ca. 1889, after the installation of the iron and brass rood screen, but before the addition of the Oberammergau reredos. Note the pulpit and sounding board on the left. The Crucifixion window over the altar was completely destroyed by the fire of 1903. *Photo by W. H. L. & Co. Courtesy, Denver Public Library, Western History Department, X25577.*

In October of 1887, Dean Hart met with three other Denver clergy: Monsignor William J. O'Ryan of St. Leo the Great Catholic Church, the Reverend Myron W. Reed of the First Congregational Church, and Rabbi William S. Friedman of Temple Emanuel. Together they formed the first community charity solicitation fund in the United States, the Denver Charity Organization Society, which later became the Community Chest and eventually the United Way.[39] In addressing the needs of Denver in 1887, these four men started a movement that is now the largest fundraising activity for charity in the world.

The ladies of the Cathedral Aid Society, ca. 1886. The first
women's organization at St. John's (originally called the Parish
Aid Society), provided service to the parish until 1930. In 1908,
the new Women's Auxiliary to the Board of Missions took over
the women's missionary work. In 1930, in the Guild Room (present
library) of the new parish house, these two organizations combined as the Women's Auxiliary; in 1960 the name changed to the
Women of St. John's. *Cathedral archives.*

Dean Hart's crusades were many. To name a few: he was for religious
training and smaller classes in the public schools, for alcohol-free bars, against
Christian Science, against the manufacture and sale of pistols, and against theat-
rical productions on Sundays. The latter prompted an article about Denver,
which appeared in the *New York Evening Post*:

> The crusade against Sunday night amusements in this city culminated
> last night in the arrest of the managers and performers in all the thea-
> tres of the city, including the Tabor Grand Theatre, where a concert
> was being given by the Hungarian Orchestra. Dean Hart of the Epis-
> copal Church has been at the head of the movement, and after the ar-
> rests had been made a mob of about 500 persons gathered, and after a
> few incendiary speeches, moved to the house of the Dean, where they
> demolished the windows and doors. Dean Hart had been told that
> the crowd was coming, and escaped by a back door, where he
> mounted a horse. The escape of the minister only served to anger the
> mob.[40]

Dean Hart reported that the newspapers greatly exaggerated the confronta-
tion—as usual.

Hart did not limit his crusades to secular matters; the Church and the
bishop were also fair game. To add fuel to the fire with the bishop, in January of
1900, the dean published a small book titled *Priestcraft, Roman and Others,* in which
he sought to show the fallacies of what he called "ritualists." This prompted the
bishop to say: "It is superficial, as all that Dean Hart says and thinks always is.
. . . He knows nothing of the theology of the Church. . . . The Dean always ar-
rogated to himself more power than he has ever been given; all he has is what I
gave him."[41] And the dean replied: "Neither do I care anything about Bishop
Spalding or what he has to say."[42]

This amazing man served for forty years as dean of St. John's and, of
course, had a number of assistants and canons during those four decades. First
were the canons appointed by Bishop Spalding and later by Bishop Olmsted to
the Cathedral Chapter as part of the cathedral system. Among these were the
principal of Jarvis Hall boys' school, the rector of Trinity Memorial Chapel, the
rector of St. Paul's in Littleton, and the president of the Standing Committee

St. John's Cathedral's second choir camp at Evergreen, 1897. *Photo from Anne Douglas, the wife of Canon Douglas. Cathedral archives.*

of the Missionary District. It is quite clear that these canons were not assistants to the dean. In fact, as the years went by, a feeling of animosity developed between the dean and at least some of the bishops' appointed canons. Over a period of about thiry-five years, the two bishops appointed many canons—as many as six residential canons and four honorary canons at one time—a practice that ceased with the reorganization of the diocese of Colorado in 1915.

From 1879 until 1892 Dean Hart had six assistants, only one of whom lasted more than a year. This frequent turnover changed when the Reverend Francis Byrne became his assistant and canon in 1892.[43] Nearly eighty-five years old at the time, Byrne had been born in Ireland in 1807, educated in Dublin, and at the age of eighteen had enlisted in the 64th Regiment of Foot [infantry]. His unit was sent to Port Royal, Jamaica, at the time a British West Indies colony. He served there for more than twelve years and was discharged in 1838 as a color sergeant but remained in Jamaica doing missionary work. He was given authority as a lay reader by Christopher, Lord Bishop of Jamaica, in 1839 and was ordained

Dr. John H. Gower, organist and choirmaster, 1887–1892. In regard to his coming, Dean Hart wrote, "Hence dates the end of our troubles and the commencement of our golden age." He had been organist at Queen Victoria's Princess Royal Chapel at Windsor. He gave up St. John's to go into mining. *Photo from program. Cathedral archives.*

The Reverend Francis Byrne, once Bishop Randall's "army of one," and later canon at the cathedral. Photo taken about the time of his retirement at age 89 in 1900. *Cathedral archives.*

St. John's Cathedral prepared for the memorial service for Queen Victoria on February 2, 1901. Note the Union Jack flags everywhere, Caledonian Club signs on pews, and initials VRA (Victoria Regina Alexandrina) on pulpit *(not readable in this photo)*. Sounding board is draped. *Photo by Joseph Collier. Courtesy, Denver Public Library, Western History Department, C194.*

deacon in 1850. Some time after settling in Massachusetts, he was convinced by Bishop Randall to come to Colorado as a missionary. Bishop Randall ordained him priest, calling Byrne his "army of one."

Over a period of twenty-five years, Byrne served churches in fourteen different towns in Colorado before coming to the cathedral. Byrne finally retired in 1900, but continued to serve the cathedral on a part-time basis for four more years. When the memorial service for Queen Victoria was held in St. John's

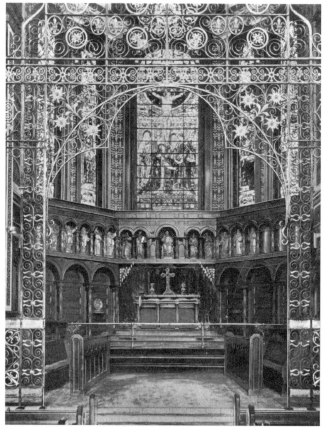

The chancel of St. John's Cathedral one week before it was burned, May 15, 1903. In the reredos, note that three figures on the right and one on the left had not yet been installed. The Bayaud memorial window was completely destroyed by the fire. *Cathedral archives.*

Cathedral in February 1901, Byrne was asked to pronounce the benediction. A Denver newspaper reported that "he never lost his pride in the fact that he had served Queen Victoria in the army and never was heard to pronounce her name without adding to it his heartfelt 'God bless her.'" He died in June 1904 at age 97; a notation in the service register in Dean Hart's hand reads, "The oldest priest in America."[44]

The morning after the fire destroyed the first cathedral, May 15, 1903. Note the reredos niches from which the carved figures were rescued. *Courtesy, Denver Public Library, Western History Department, F8275.*

Bishop Spalding died in 1902 and was succeeded by Bishop Charles Sanford Olmsted. Just two weeks after Bishop Olmsted's consecration, a tragedy occurred. According to Dean Hart: "A miscreant set fire to the old Cathedral on Friday night, May 15, 1903."[45] Denver newspapers reported that the interior of the cathedral was completely destroyed. Despite these reports, all the windows were saved except the great East window. The baptismal font, the rood screen, and the reredos were also saved, although the latter suffered some fire damage. According to a historical sketch by Dr. Robert L. Stearns in 1927, the "dear old Dean" had carried practically all the carvings from the burning building on his own back. It was also reported that the dean personally directed the fire fighting.[46]

As Dean Hart surveyed the ruins of the cathedral the next morning, it is likely that his thoughts were already turning to a new and greater cathedral. He immediately published the following notice:

> My Dear Friends—Nothing could exceed the depths of universal sympathy which the loss of our beautiful church has evoked. . . . We have finally concluded to hold our early communion at 7:30 every Sunday morning in Central Presbyterian Church. . . . As all our books are soaked, we will not have any mid-day service tomorrow, but for the future we have accepted the kind loan of the Jewish synagogue[47] at the corner of 16th and Pearl Streets, wherein to hold our 11 o'clock service and the Sunday school at 3 o'clock. . . . Cast down, but not destroyed.[48]

Immediately after the fire, the vestry offered a reward of one thousand dollars for the apprehension and conviction of the person who set the fire. The arsonist was never found, but it is likely that it was someone who was more than a little upset with the dean. Later one of the newspapers reported the dean as saying:

> We haven't caught the fellow who set fire to the cathedral. There were some clues, but they developed nothing. When the chap that did it gets into the other world, he'll preach against hell-fire, I warrant you.[49]

Temple Emanuel, the Jewish synagogue where St. John's held services in 1903–1904. Sold in 1957, it is now the Temple Events Center. Photo taken before the 1924 enlargement. *Courtesy, Colorado Historical Society, S25653.*

3. *The Great Dean and the Second Cathedral, 1903–1920*

WITH THE OLD CATHEDRAL LOST, DEAN HART immediately began to plan for a new and greater cathedral. First was the question of location. The prevailing sentiment of the congregation favored building the new cathedral on Capitol Hill, at that time the finest residential area of Denver. By the end of June 1903, the half block bounded by 14th Avenue, Washington and Clarkson streets was purchased. Across Clarkson Street, on the site of the present Morey Middle School, stood Wolfe Hall, the Episcopal girls' school.

Soon a circular announcing a "Competition for a church building to be erected in the City of Denver" was sent to eight architects, offering $150 as incentive for their designs. Other architects also applied until eighteen architects

Wolfe Hall, the Episcopal girls' school on Clarkson Street between 13th and 14th avenues. The school, started in 1868 at 17th and Champa streets, built this building in 1885. The school closed in 1913, and the building was sold to the Denver Public Schools in 1920. *Photo by L. C. McClure. Courtesy, Denver Public Library, Western History Department, MCC4209.*

submitted a total of nineteen designs; six were from Colorado, two from London, and the rest from various eastern states. As the result of the recommendation of a consulting architect, the design for a Late Gothic Revival (English) building submitted by the New York firm of Tracy & Swartwout was chosen as winner of the competition.[50]

To provide temporary quarters for the congregation, Tracy & Swartwout designed a chapter house,[51] which was completed under the direction of a local architect in August of 1904. This white brick, Romanesque structure was located on Clarkson Street facing Wolfe Hall, where the Roberts Education and Music

The winning design by Tracy & Swartwout, New York. Watercolor concept developed by the architects. *Cathedral archives.*

Building now stands. It was fitted with eleven of the windows salvaged from the old cathedral, as well as the reredos and carved figures, some of which had not yet been installed when the fire occurred. The chapter house was used for church services for seven years. Because of its small seating capacity of 500 (with 100 spaces reserved for the girls from Wolfe Hall), many of the members of the parish relocated to other churches. It was during the latter part of these seven years that, for the only time in its history, St. John's was not the largest Episcopal congregation in Denver.[52]

It was soon apparent that the cost of building the winning design would far exceed the $125,000 limit set forth in the competition. Tracy & Swartwout were told to modify the design and prepare working drawings. The design was for the complete cathedral; the working drawings were for the "church," the name given to the cathedral nave and a temporary chancel. The modified design for the cathedral was received in July 1904, but the working drawings were not

The north end of
the chapter house
when used for
church services
from 1904 to 1911.
Cathedral archives.

forthcoming. At the urging of Dean Hart, Tracy & Swartwout provided drawings for the foundation, which was soon completed under a local architect's direction. By this time the working drawings had arrived and bids indicated that
building this second design would still cost $300,000, more than twice the
amount allowed. The building committee again rejected the plans and called on
Tracy & Swartwout to submit new plans that would comply with the terms of
the competition. The low bid on the third design, $160,000, was more than
planned for, but the building committee did not want to start over again. The
following claim, found within a statement from the Ways and Means Committee, was advanced to stimulate fundraising:

> The plans and specifications furnished by the architects and adopted
> by the trustees of St. John's will, if carried out, result in placing a
> building in our city that will have no equal in the United States out-
> side of New York City, and would be a credit and honor to any city in
> America.[53]

The second
design by Tracy &
Swartwout, New
York, 1904.
*Watercolor concept
developed by the
architects. Cathedral
archives.*

The working drawings finally arrived in late 1907, and construction began in 1908. Although the original plans called for building the cathedral with
Colorado marble, no quarry could be found that was adequately developed to
insure a sufficient quantity of uniform stone. For this reason, and because it
would save about $3,500, it was decided to use oolite limestone from Bedford,
Indiana. The cornerstone of the Cathedral of Saint John the Evangelist was
placed by Bishop Olmsted on January 24, 1909.

By Labor Day, September 5, 1909, the towers were almost completed and
the walls and clerestory were nearly to the roofline. The contractor, Arvid Olsen,
inspecting the building alone after a heavy rain, discovered that one of the pillars was cracked and several of the pillars had settled and thrown the clerestory
out of line. All construction ceased. It was soon determined that the foundation
piers were not large enough or placed deeply enough to bear the weight of the
pillars. In the redesign of the nave, the configuration of flying buttresses that

Service leaflet for the laying of the foundation stone of the second cathedral, January 24, 1909. *Cathedral archives.*

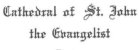

Cathedral of St. John the Evangelist

Denver

THE OFFICE FOR THE

Laying of the Foundation Stone

✠

Third Sunday after the Epiphany, January 24th, A. D. 1909

Bishop Olmsted at the laying of cornerstone for the new cathedral on January 24, 1909. *Cathedral archives.*

Inside the nave, the builders of the cathedral sit on the platform of the steam-driven crane, which ran on railroad tracks inside the structure, 1909. *Courtesy, Denver Public Library, Western History Department, F42572.*

Construction of the cathedral in 1909, with the crane protruding above the walls. Office of A. Olson, contractor, in foreground. *Photo by L. C. McClure. Courtesy, Denver Public Library, Western History Department, MCC3800.*

The brand new Cathedral of Saint John the Evangelist, ca. 1912. *Cathedral archives.*

would have spread the weight of the clerestory and roof to the outside had been replaced with a plan in which the inside pillars supported all of the weight. After five months' debate, it was decided to dismiss Tracy & Swartwout and to take down the walls, the sixteen pillars and all they supported, and to rebuild the foundation. The disassembly, repairs, and rebuilding created a delay of a year and a half at a cost of $30,000. The nave and temporary chancel were then finished without further incident. The first service in the new Cathedral of Saint John the Evangelist was held on November 5, 1911. Nine decades later the cathedral is still not completed: the main tower, choir, and two transepts are yet to be built.[54]

    It was during 1910 to 1911 that the much-reported meeting between Dean Hart and Bishop Matz occurred. St. John's Cathedral and the Roman Catholic

Interior of St. John's Cathedral, ca. 1912. Note the pulpit and the lectern with their soundboards and stairways from the nave. Also, there is no gap in the rows of pews to make a crossing. The apse windows were replaced in the 1960s. *Photo by L. C. McClure. Courtesy, Denver Public Library, Western History Department, MCC2033.*

Cathedral[55] were under construction at the same time. In 1929, W. W. Grant Jr., one-time vestry member of St. John's, spoke of the meeting:

> Dean Hart's encounter with Bishop Matz when the foundations of this cathedral cracked is typical. One of the spires of Bishop Matz's cathedral had recently been struck by lighting. The two chanced to meet and Bishop Matz said, "I see your church is caved in. I always thought there was something wrong with your foundations." The Dean replied, "Well, Bishop, our troubles may be from below, but yours are from above."[56]

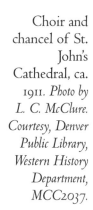

Choir and chancel of St. John's Cathedral, ca. 1911. *Photo by L. C. McClure. Courtesy, Denver Public Library, Western History Department, MCC2037.*

Entering the new cathedral from 14th Avenue, parishioners were met with the carved stone heads of St. John the Evangelist and Mary the Madonna. According to the *Denver Post,* "Dean Hart's face looks down from St. John's statue"; the models for the sculptures were Dean Hart and his daughter Margaret. The *Post* continues, "despite the streamers of long hair the likeness of statue to model is startlingly clear."[57] Just inside the doors, in the vestibule—called the narthex—two stones were placed in the walls. When Dean Hart was at the Pan-Anglican Conference in 1908, he asked his friends Dean Wace of Canterbury Cathedral and Dean Robinson of Westminster Abbey to donate stones from their cathedrals to be imbedded in the walls of St. John's Cathedral. The stones arrived and, according to Dean Hart, they are part of "the Church's One Foundation."[58]

Dean Hart wrote in his book *Recollections and Reflections,* "One morning I met Mr. George Schleier on the street. He told me he wished to present the ca-

Dean Hart's campanile (belfry). On the left is the chapter house and on the right, across the street, is Wolfe Hall. *Photo from "The Bells of St. John's Cathedral," 1906, by H. Martyn Hart. Cathedral archives.*

thedral with a peal of bells and he gave me carte blanche to get the best I could." Dean Hart had the bells cast by Petit, Edelbrock, & Co. at Gescher, a small town near Cologne in Germany. He went to Gescher to inspect them and found that "they were all in perfect tune as they came from their molds, that is, they were 'maiden' bells."[59] The bells arrived in Denver in 1905 before construction started on the cathedral, so they were installed in a wooden campanile located near where the Common Room is now. This was a seventy-foot high belfry that looked a bit oriental. The headlines of one Denver newspaper read, "Don't call Dean Hart's building a 'Pagoda,' it's a 'Campanile.'"[60] The fifteen bells were hung in the cathedral towers in 1911, fourteen in the west tower; only the clappers move when they are rung from a clavitur, or console, at the balcony level. The tenor bell, which weighs 9,240 pounds, hangs alone in the east tower; originally designed to swing, it now is also fixed.

Dean Hart had great plans for the windows of the cathedral, and he originally meant for the Frampton Studios, which had made the windows for the first cathedral to do them all. A letter from Edward Frampton confirms that intention: "The Dean wrote me when he had the designs for the new Cathedral settled, saying, 'I intend to try and live to build this Cathedral, and I want you to live to fill it with stained glass.'"[61] Hart envisioned that over the entrance would be the Last Judgment window; the west aisle would illustrate the History of Sin; the east aisle, the History of Salvation; the clerestory, the History of the Church; and the temporary apse would hold the windows from the old cathedral, featuring the Ascension. With money given to him by his parishioners on the occasion of his birthday in 1912, the dean paid for the first window in the west aisle in memory of his wife. This fascinating window depicts Eve in the Garden of Eden with a "very English" lion looking on. In *The Stained Glass Windows of St. John's Cathedral*, 1990, Gladys Alexander writes, "Eve is somewhat obscured by a thigh-high rose bush, purported to have been added later due to the prudish reaction of the well-covered Edwardian congregation" (p. 4). The Last Judgment window was soon installed. By this time, England was in the throes of World War I, and the window contains a small inscription, "This great window finished and fixed in the year of the great Armageddon—of the Apocalypse—October 1914 Miserere Domine."[62]

Several other aisle windows were ordered from Frampton; but soon Dean Hart and Edward Frampton had disagreements over the costs of the windows. It is obvious from his correspondence that Frampton felt the dean had promised him more windows if the great west ["ecclesiastically" west, but it is actually north] window was satisfactory. He also indicated that the dean had written him saying that the window was beautiful beyond his expectations. It was not the quality of the work, but a matter of money that came between

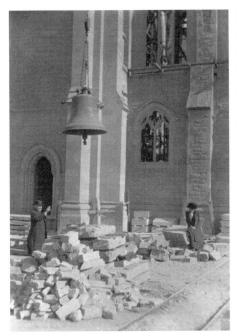

Dean Hart watching the raising of the bishop's bell (fourteenth bell) to the west tower during construction of the cathedral, 1911. *Cathedral archives.*

Dean Hart at the console of the old organ, and his daughter, Margaret, about 1912. (Note that the console was on the east side of the choir. The aisle windows and the north portal window contained plain glass.) *Cathedral archives.*

The Last Judgment window over the west (north) portal, given in 1912 as a memorial to Charles Brewer Kountze, founder of the Colorado National Bank and a member of St. John's for forty-seven years. The window was finished by Edward Frampton of London, in 1914. It was seriously damaged in 1967 by earthquakes and again in 1990 by hail. *Photo by Robert E. Harris. Cathedral archives.*

Eve in the Garden of Eden window, given in memory of Eleanor Hart. *Cathedral archives.*

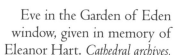

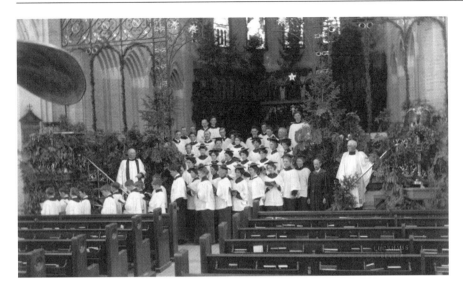

St. John's choir at Christmastime, ca. 1916. Dean Hart is on the left and Henry Houseley (black robe), choirmaster, and Rector Emeritus Hitchings are on the right. Note the parabolic sounding board above the pulpit and the two stairways to the pulpit on the left and the lectern on the right. *Photo by Luckhaus, Denver. Cathedral archives.*

them. Frampton wrote that because of the unsettled war conditions, no one in England was ordering stained-glass windows, and his future depended on anticipated orders from St. John's. Hart then ordered the first two clerestory windows from competitors of Frampton, one in London and the other in New York. These windows, installed in the south end of the east clerestory, depict the Oxford Martyrs and the presentations of the English Bible and Prayer Book. Frampton was furious, the long-time association was broken, and soon the Frampton studios ceased to exist.

Dean Hart was well known for his sermons, always written out by hand, with most later published in little booklets for distribution and many appearing in the Denver newspapers. Many of his sermons reflected his strong feelings on social issues. His scrapbook contains a letter commenting on one of his sermons:

> Reverend and Dear Sir,
>
> I was greatly pleased to read in the News this morning your powerful sermon delivered yesterday in your Church, and I hasten to congratulate you for having the courage and ability to proclaim the truth from your pulpit to the top of Society as you do. It is warnings and proclamations of the truth such as your sermon that we greatly need if we are to be saved from the consequences of our own follies, greed, and sin. More strength to your elbow dear Dean, and God bless you.
>
> Respectfully and Sincerely
> Yours, Lars P. Nelson.[63]

Always a man ahead of this time, by 1904 Dean Hart had an automobile dubbed Betty, a gift from his congregation in celebration of the twenty-fifth anniversary of his ministry at St. John's. At the time he said, "My old horse was getting whiter and whiter and slower and slower. Now the beast can have a good rest which it deserves." The automobile was a one-cylinder Cadillac and became the talk of the town. When the congregation replaced this car twelve years later, the gift prompted the following newspaper article:

> Any resident who has been two or more years in Denver will remember that Dean H. Martyn Hart of St. John's Cathedral used to own a prehistoric device of antediluvian mechanism and aboriginal aspect, which was known as "Dean Hart's Car." Nothing else would describe it for the name of the maker was lost in the dim reaches of the past and it looked like no other mechanical conveyance extant.

"Professor" Henry Houseley came to Denver from Nottingham, England, in 1888 as deputy organist and became organist and choirmaster in 1892. He was also organist at Temple Emanuel and occasionally at St. Mark's and Oakes Home. He was a prolific composer and director and formed the first community symphony orchestra in Denver in 1900. Following his death in 1925, his ashes were interred in the east wall of the choir. *Cathedral archives.*

On the front steps of the new cathedral, ca. 1915. Left to right: Adams Owen, bass soloist for twenty-three years; William Yardley, sexton and verger for twenty-nine years; Dean Hart; and Henry Houseley, organist and choirmaster for thirty-seven years. *Cathedral archives.*

Dean Hart in front of the old cloister between the cathedral and the chapter house, 1914. *Cathedral archives.*

Today the Dean longs with all his heart that he might get the old car back. Yesterday someone drove away with Dean Hart's new car. Until it was found late last night the household at 1324 Washington was upset. Again the Dean reflected this would not have happened had he been faithful to "Betty." No man North of Pueblo would drive away with "Betty." The Dean, it is said, contemplates returning to the vehicle that stood by him for fifteen years.[64]

Although beloved by his congregation, in the years following the completion of the new cathedral, it became obvious that the relationship between Dean Hart and Bishop Olmsted left much to be desired. Hart, an evangelical (low) churchman, did object to the bishop's high churchship, but the main problem was the unbelievable financial chaos that the bishop had allowed the diocese

H. Martyn Hart, the "Great Dean" as he approached his last years, in 1917. *Cathedral archives.*

to fall into. This culminated when the diocesan chapter clerk confessed embezzlement, and the bishop left town. He spent several years in Saybrook, Connecticut, while the diocese was managed by the Standing Committee. During this time the diocese was reorganized and the Bishop and Chapter organization was replaced by an organization that provided for a board of trustees.

The headline of a 1915 Denver newspaper read: "Dean Hart at last decides to be American. Desire to be bishop is said to be reason for unexpected action." Hart had been criticized for thirty-five years for his refusal to renounce allegiance to King George V of Great Britain, and because he still bought his clerical clothes abroad. Dean Hart countered, "I don't see that the change will make the slightest difference beyond allaying prejudice. I have no desire and no intention of becoming a bishop."[65] He became an American citizen on April 7, 1919.

Irving Peake Johnson, third bishop of Colorado, 1918–1938. *Cathedral archives.*

In 1916 a bishop coadjutor, nominated by the dean, was elected. Several years later Dean Paul Roberts wrote about this situation in *The Open Door* (the weekly bulletin of St. John's):

> Bishop Johnson was consecrated January 1, 1917. He came at a time when the diocese was in a state of disorganization, both temporally and spiritually. He faced the forbidding task of reviving the spiritual life of the Church, of inspiring the clergy, of reenlisting the laity, of assuming responsibility for an extensive missionary district. With

executive ability rarely found in a cleric, with qualities of leadership that compel all to follow willingly and cheerfully, with wisdom, godliness, and tremendous spiritual power, he has, during the past twenty years, led the Church in Colorado to a high plane of spiritual life and temporal efficiency. [66]

Bishop Olmsted died in October 1918, and Bishop Johnson became the diocesan bishop. Dean Hart's last years were served under Bishop Irving P. Johnson, a bishop beloved by all, including the dean.

Sometime after the completion of the new cathedral, the parish proceeded to initiate a lawsuit against the architects, alleging that they were responsible for the settling of the foundation and the cost of rebuilding. The argument dragged on for years. The key question seemed to be whether the local architect worked for Tracy & Swartwout or for Saint John's Church in the Wilderness. The *Denver Times* reported in March of 1920, "Against the advice of those who were aware of the dangers of a long journey, Dean Hart left Denver on Monday, January 26 for New York where he desired to testify in a suit brought by the Cathedral against Tracy & Swartwout."

On his return to Denver the dean contracted pneumonia. On the morning of March 24, 1920, at age 82, the Very Reverend H. Martyn Hart died in the deanery[67] and was buried beside Mr. Hitchings (an earlier rector) next to the east wall of the cathedral. His body lay in state in the cathedral for five hours before the funeral, and hundreds of people paid their respects.

Hart had been rector of Saint John's Church in the Wilderness and dean of the cathedral for forty years. His scrapbook, finished by his daughter after his death, has page after page of newspaper articles about his life and his ministry. Despite his lifelong conflict with the press, the obituaries and articles written at the time of his death were all testimonials to his greatness. A Denver attorney wrote to the dean's daughter on March 26:

Celtic cross given in 1918 by the Horace B. Hitchings estate following his burial. This photo taken after Dean Hart's burial in 1920. *Cathedral archives.*

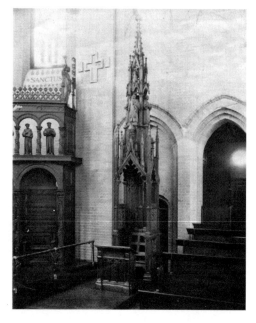

The cathedra (bishop's seat and prie-dieu) given by the Hitchings estate in 1918, a replica of the bishop's throne of Worcester Cathedral, England. The figures on the superstructure are the Reverend Horace B. Hitchings, rector, 1862–1868; Bishop George M. Randall, missionary bishop and rector, 1868–1873; and Bishop Franklin S. Spalding, missionary bishop of Utah and the son of Bishop John Franklin Spalding, first bishop of Colorado. Note the old brass altar rail and old choir stalls and the position of the cathedra in front of the door. The cathedra was moved behind the new altar rail in December 1948. *Cathedral archives.*

Deanery at 1324 Washington Street, demolished in 1975 when the Diocesan Center was built. *Cathedral archives.*

The cathedral nearing completion. This photo was used as plaintiff's exhibit in 1920. The penciled line descending from the tower indicates the extent of construction when the structure needed to be pulled down. The accented arches and the X'd pier indicate the area of major damage. Note Dean Hart in his automobile dubbed Betty in the foreground. *Cathedral archives.*

The "Great Dean" leaves his cathedral. *Cathedral archives.*

Mrs. Hanington;

As a friend joined me the other morning, he said: Dean Hart is dead. At those words, I felt the uttermost sense of loneliness.

I went back, in memory, to that Sabbath evening, in November 1881, when I first heard the Dean; I was a homesick boy, just come to the great, gray, lonesome plains, and from that night I was comforted, refreshed and encouraged by the most earnest, brilliant and logical pulpit presentation of the verities of life, that I had ever listened to.

As the years followed on, he united me in marriage to my wife; he performed for her family the last services and to us he was a refuge in every trial of life.

It seemed to me at first that Denver could no longer be Denver, with the Dean departed; and yet, he was so forciful [*sic*], so earnest, so courageous, that his memory is a continuing force.

The valiant soldier of the cross; the great knight templar has passed from the church militant to the church triumphant, and he walks with the mighty men of redemption that are the consummation lights of the world.

When I reflect upon the work that he has done; the church that he has builded, there comes to mind the words of the prophet who, looking from the tops of the rocks and the high hills, on to the works of the patriarch Jacob, exclaimed, "Let me die the death of the righteous; let my last end be like his."

Very faithfully in the common
sorrow of us all, Caesar A. Roberts

Canon Winfred Douglas wrote sixteen years later:

> Of the great Dean, one remembers first of all his intense vitality and
> energy, his practical good sense, his wonderful care for the sick and
> needy, his profoundly deep and simple piety. He was generally up at
> five, and after a cup of tea, worked on those truly evangelical sermons
> which changed so many lives. They were always written out in full, and
> read from the manuscript: but read in so vivid a manner as not to lose
> directness in the least. His standards of reading divine service were of
> the highest; and woe to that curate who fell into indistinctness or
> sloppiness in the chancel. No one will ever forget the devotion, the
> reverence, the dignity, which were shown by Dean Hart at Holy Com-
> munion. . . . With the passing of Dean Hart to his eternal reward, the
> old days were finished.[68]

Dean Hart did not live to see the end of the conflict with Tracy &
Swartwout. A few months after his death, the cathedral lost the lawsuit to the
architects; and in addition to having to pay for the reconstruction of the cathedral, damages were awarded equal to the commission the architects would
have earned if they had completed the cathedral.

4. Dean Browne, 1921–1924

FOR THE FIFTEEN MONTHS FOLLOWING DEAN HART'S DEATH, the Reverend Frank Frederick Beckerman, canon of the cathedral, admirably fulfilled the duties of interim pastor and rector.[69] During this period the vestry considered several candidates for dean, including a young priest named Henry Knox Sherrill, but decided not to call them. Some twenty-five years later, the Reverend Sherrill was elected presiding bishop of the Episcopal Church in America.

In March of 1921, the Reverend Duncan H. Browne, D.D., rector of Christ Church on Staten Island, New York, was called to be rector of Saint John's Church in the Wilderness and dean of the cathedral. He was instituted rector and installed dean in October of 1921. Forty-two years old at the time of his election, he had lived all his life in New York, graduating from Columbia University and Union Theological Seminary. As an army chaplain during World

Frontier stagecoach that met Daniel S. Tuttle, presiding bishop, at Denver Union
Station, 1921. Bishop Tuttle had first come to Denver fifty-four years earlier in a
similar coach. Standing is the Reverend Frederick Oaks, who would act as master
of ceremonies at the consecration of Bishop Fred Ingley on June 11, 1921. In
the coach are Bishop-elect Ingley and Canon Sherman Coolidge, the Native
American clergyman. *Cathedral archives.*

War I, he had won the Distinguished Service Cross at the battle of Argonne
Forrest in 1918. At his institution service, Bishop Johnson said in his sermon:

> You are come to us highly commended as one who has been coura-
> geous in danger, resourceful in need, kindly in service to men, reverent

Captain Duncan
H. Browne,
chaplain, 305th
Infantry, U.S.
Army. *Photo from
St. John's service
leaflet, May 1, 1921.
Cathedral archives.*

in worship to God. . . . To this congregation I do not doubt you will
prove a faithful pastor, a courageous prophet, a godly priest and a wise
administrator.[70]

Perhaps he was all of these things, but a review of the vestry minutes during his
tenure reveal a most uneventful period. It was nearly impossible to fill the shoes
of a "great dean."

At the time Browne became dean of the cathedral, four of the west aisle
windows were still to be filled. According to Dean Hart's plan they were reserved for the History of Sin, and sin was apparently a hard sell. At the vestry
meeting on October 10, 1921, "It was moved and carried that windows nos. 5, 6,
7, & 8 on the west aisle be no longer held exclusively for the events of the history of Amalek [descendents of Esau as provided in the original scheme for the
windows]."[71] Within a few years these windows were filled with New Testament

The Tiffany window given in memory of Eleanor Baxter. The window was saved from the fire in 1903 and installed in the present cathedral in 1921. *Cathedral archives.*

themes. Sometime after the death of Dean Hart a small semicircular window was installed over the front doors in the cathedral narthex. Correspondence between a parishioner and Dean Browne in 1923 indicates that the window "placed over the door some years ago" is the same window saved from the fire in 1903. This gem of a window, a child holding a lily against the cross, was designed by Harris Stevenson of Boston and made by Tiffany & Co. It was originally given in 1889 in memory of Eleanor Baxter, a child who had died in 1885.

By December of 1921, the vestry was confronted by the poor financial condition of the parish, and in the minutes we find:

Duncan Hodge Browne, the second dean of St. John's Cathedral, 1921–1924. *Cathedral archives.*

It was the sense of the Vestry, with regrets, that the present financial condition of the Parish did not warrant retaining the services of Canon F. F. Beckerman who had proven himself to be a faithful and loyal man in the hour of trial of this Church.[72]

By mutual agreement, Canon Beckerman resigned, effective January 15, 1922. In spite of this poor financial condition, the vestry purchased the six lots at the corner of 13th Avenue and Clarkson Street, thus completing the block. It took four years to pay for them. Under Browne's direction the old "red" prayer books were replaced with the "standard" prayer books, the cathedral began the use of the new Authorized Church Hymnal, and for the first time wafers were used at communion rather than unleavened bread.

In March of 1924, Dean Browne accepted what he referred to as an "urgent call" from Chicago's oldest parish, St. James Church, and again, so soon, St. John's was looking for a new rector and dean. For three months following Dean Browne's departure, the cathedral was in the care of Chaplain Ernest Wetherill Wood, United States Army, who was stationed at Fort Logan. Ultimately the vestry looked to Pueblo, only eighty miles south, to replace Dean Browne.

5. Dagwell: Rector, Dean, and Bishop, 1924–1936

THE NEXT RECTOR AND DEAN WAS BENJAMIN DUNLAP DAGWELL. Born in 1890 in Susquehannah, Pennsylvania, Dagwell was educated at the University of Cincinnati, Seabury Divinity School, and General Theological Seminary, and ordained to the diaconate in 1916 and to the priesthood in 1917. He was rector of St. Mary's Church in Keyport, New Jersey, before being called as rector of the Church of the Ascension in Pueblo in 1920. He had served there for four years when the vestry of St. John's called him to be rector and dean on April 15, 1924. In an unusual letter to the wife of St. John's junior warden, written a few days later, he said: "I want you as unkind friends who will help me by merciless and constructive criticism. I have many limitations and feel almost presumptuous in

The young Benjamin Dunlap Dagwell, ca. 1924, the third dean of St. John's Cathedral. *Cathedral archives.*

accepting so great a work as has been offered me."[73] He began his duties at St. John's within the month. It was a thirty-four-year-old and very eligible bachelor who was instituted rector of Saint John's Church in the Wilderness and installed dean of St. John's Cathedral on September 28, 1924, by Bishop Irving P. Johnson.

St. John's Cathedral immediately began to thrive under the direction of Dean Dagwell. The debt on the building of the cathedral was paid, and the building was finally consecrated on June 11, 1925. Presiding Bishop Ethelbert Talbot preached, and Bishop Johnson chose for the Sentence of Consecration the words that Bishop Joseph Cruikshank Talbot[74] had used for the first little church on Arapahoe Street in 1862. The Sentence of Consecration, signed by Bishop Johnson, and read at this service by Dean Dagwell said, "I do hereby consecrate and set apart this building, by the name and title of Saint John's Church in the Wilderness; solemnly dedicating it to the memory of Saint John the Baptist." Bishop Johnson's words added to the confusion about the name of St. John's: the building named the Cathedral of Saint John the Evangelist, which was owned by the congregation named Saint John's Church in the Wilderness, was consecrated to the memory of Saint John the Baptist.[75]

Less than a year after Dagwell's arrival, in his first annual report to the parish, he stated:

> When I first met with the Vestry, I was promised that when I created the demand, the plant and equipment would be provided. Well, the demand has been created, the business has been secured. The Chapter House is outgrown. . . . We must either curtail our work, or have enlarged facilities. . . . I propose, too, that the Diocesan offices should be located in this [new] building. . . . How is all this to be accomplished? Well, that is your affair. My task is to provide the business. Yours is to furnish the materials.[76]

Thus began the plans for a new parish house. The architectural firm of Merrill and Burnham Hoyt was retained to design the new parish house.[77]

Construction began in November of 1926 and was completed in September of 1927. The building originally had the dean's and canons' offices, reception area, chapel, dining hall, and kitchen on the first floor; the bishops' offices and the women's guild room on the second floor; and fourteen classrooms and a library on the third floor. Prior to building this parish house, some of the offices of the clergy and parish were situated in the deanery (the dean's residence that faced Washington Street), and the diocesan offices were located in a downtown office building. In August, the vestry had authorized Dean Dagwell

The chapter house, ca. 1925. Used for offices, meeting rooms, Sunday School, and the choir. On the left is the cloister leading to the cathedral. This view is looking east from outside the south end of the cathedral. The Paul Roberts building occupies this site today. *Photo by Colorado Photo Co. Cathedral archives.*

to move to the Olin Hotel so that the deanery could be used for the church school during the construction period.

In 1921, Elisabeth Spalding, daughter of Bishop Spalding, and Marion Hendrie persuaded the diocese of Colorado to constitute a Commission on Church Architecture and the Allied Arts to encourage and guide parishes and missions in obtaining the best possible design in buildings and furnishings.

When St. John's undertook the building of St. Martin's Chapel and the parish house in 1926, Dean Dagwell placed the responsibility for the design of the chapel in the hands of the art commission. After the chapel's completion the commission prepared a little booklet in which they stated:

> Because the members of the Commission of Architecture and the Allied Arts of the Diocese of Colorado feel strongly that the work planned by an individual artist for a definite place has a greater spiritual content than work produced in quantity, they have sought cooperation with artists in the building of Saint Martin's Chapel. Denver is unusually fortunate in having artists of international recognition, and it is conceded that their thought and effort have created a chapel of great spiritual and artistic beauty.[78]

The dominant work is the reredos, given by Mrs. Hendrie for "The Children of Saint John's Cathedral." The artist was Arnold Rönnebeck,[79] at the time head of the Denver Art Museum. The chapel was dedicated to St. Martin of Tours on November 11, 1927. Dean Barrall wrote about the chapel in 1968:

> Saint Martin's Chapel is widely known and appreciated as representing an unusual combination of both old and newer religious art and architectural forms. When the chapel was completed in 1928, it was thought by many to be extreme, for its modern adaptations were far beyond the contemporary usage of that day. Today the chapel appears modern and relevant—but not extreme. In contrast to many present-day church buildings, it is actually conservative![80]

The chapel was originally meant to be a children's chapel, but over the years it has become a favorite of the adults in the congregation. It is used frequently for baptisms, weddings, and funerals and has been the location of services in the Dakota Indian and Japanese languages.

Interior of St. Martin's Chapel, ca. 1970. Designed by the Commission of Architecture and the Allied Arts of the Diocese of Colorado. *Cathedral archives.*

The demand that Dean Dagwell created not only required enlarged facilities but also an enlarged staff. He added several assistants, two of whom made significant contributions to the life of the Episcopal Church in Colorado. The first of these was Canon Harry Watts, an Englishman, born in 1890 and educated at Seabury Divinity School. He had been rector of St. Peter's Church in West Denver and of Trinity Church in Greeley before coming to the cathedral

In progress, the reredos for St. Martin's Chapel, designed by Arnold Rönnebeck, carved by John R. Henderson, at Chappell House, Denver Art Museum, in 1927. *Courtesy, Denver Public Library, Western History Department, F42558.*

The altar in St. Martin's Chapel. The Greek phrase translates, "We have beheld His Glory" (John 1:14). *Cathedral archives.*

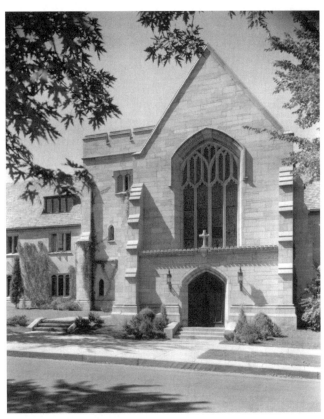

East entrance of St. Martin's Chapel, ca. 1929. Steps at left lead to the entrance of the parish house. "My house shall be called of all nations the house of prayer" is carved in the frieze surmounted by the cross. *Cathedral archives.*

in 1925. He is best remembered as being founder and vicar of St. Michael and All Angels Church on south University Boulevard, serving there as vicar from 1925 until 1928 while also being canon of the cathedral. Canon Watts continued serving the cathedral until 1959 and thereafter as canon emeritus until his death in 1986, a total of sixty years under five deans. The second assistant of note was Canon Charles Winfred Douglas, who was born in New York, received a bachelor of music degree from Syracuse University, and attended St. Andrew's Divin-

St. John's choir, ca. 1926. On the left are Carl Williams, crucifer, Dean Dagwell, and an unidentified verger. Clergy on the right are canons Sherman Coolidge, Harry Watts, and Jonathan Watson. The first man on the left in the third row is Karl Staps, choirmaster. *Photo by Mile High Photo. Cathedral archives.*

ity School, and was ordained deacon in 1893. His ministry in New York was cut short by serious lung disease, and he came to Colorado for relief. Dean Hart appointed him minor canon in 1894. He moved to Evergreen in 1896 and helped found the Mission of the Transfiguration. He briefly attended Matthew's Hall seminary in Denver and was ordained priest in 1899. During the 1920s, he and

Karl Otto Staps, organist and choirmaster from 1925–1938, came to St. John's after serving St. Paul's Church, Cincinnati. *Cathedral archives.*

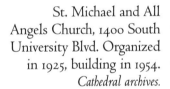

St. Michael and All Angels Church, 1400 South University Blvd. Organized in 1925, building in 1954. *Cathedral archives.*

his wife established the Evergreen Conference Center and the School of Church Music.[81] In 1934 he returned to the cathedral as honorary canon, in which post he would remain for ten years. He was one of the great musical authorities in the Episcopal Church and was the music editor for the *Hymnal* 1940. He died in 1944. Although Dean Dagwell followed the traditions of his two predecessors, Dean Hart and Dean Browne, and was called "evangelical" or "low church," both of these assistants were "Anglo-Catholic" or "high church."

In spite of the Great Depression, it was an energetic St. John's Cathedral that hosted the Fiftieth Triennial General Convention of the Episcopal Church in September of 1931. The 150 members of the House of Bishops met in the State Capitol Senate Chamber, clerical and lay delegates met in the Scottish Rite Cathedral,[82] and the women met at Central Presbyterian Church. One of

Lace altar cloth made from donations of family laces from fifty members of the cathedral, dedicated on March 31, 1929. This memorial altar cloth was used on a regular basis until the 1960s, then only for festival occasions for another twenty years. *Cathedral archives.*

Decorations for an elaborate, but unknown, wedding, ca. 1930. *Photo by Lindevall. Cathedral archives.*

the interesting things at this convention was the presentation of the 1928 *Book of Common Prayer,* which had been approved at the previous convention. St. John's Cathedral was the site of the convention's closing service.

A splendid apocryphal story about Dean Dagwell concerns the rood screen that separates the nave from the choir and chancel in the cathedral: it is told that Dean Dagwell did not like the bright brass of the rood screen that had been saved from the old cathedral, so one night he stole into the cathedral and painted the screen black—no small job—which it has remained to this day. Dean Dagwell was also responsible for the initial contact with the Connick Stained Glass Studios and the subsequent plan for the clerestory windows in the cathedral. The design provided by Connick abandoned the old English-style windows and the original plan of Dean Hart. The Connick windows would be French Gothic and the plan was Old Testament (Creation, Women, Moses, Children, Kings, Benedicite, Priests, and Prophets) on the west and Youth, Power (founders of the early church), Mercy (miracles of healing), Love (children of the New Testament), Wisdom (parables), and Majesty (Te Deum) on the east.[83] The predominant color of the windows would be blue rather than yellow. However, only one of these windows was installed during the time Dagwell was dean of the cathedral.

In November of 1935, the congregation (and especially the single ladies) of St. John's was devastated to learn that Dean Dagwell, still an eligible bachelor, had been elected bishop of Oregon. His election had come after more than a dozen ballots in the middle of the night. In the service leaflet the next week, he wrote about the call, "I am frank to tell you (and Oregon) that personal inclination was to remain here . . . the call of duty seemed stronger in Oregon . . . I have accepted the election." Benjamin Dagwell resigned as rector and dean as of January 1936, and St. John's was again searching for a new dean.[84]

Dean Dagwell, 1935, taken about the time he was elected bishop of Oregon. *Photo by Lainson. Cathedral archives.*

6. *The Dean of Humanity,*
1936–1957

FOR THE SECOND TIME THE VESTRY OF ST. JOHN'S went only a few miles south to find a new rector and dean, Paul Roberts, rector of Grace and St. Stephen's Church in Colorado Springs. Roberts was born in Newark, New Jersey, on August 3, 1887, one of four children of the Reverend and Mrs. William Roberts, natives of Wales and New England, respectively. His father died when he was two, and he and his two brothers and sister were reared in his mother's family home in Hartford, Connecticut. A graduate of Trinity College in Hartford in 1909, he had been a member of the football and track teams and was captain of the hockey team. In his senior year he realized that he was going to follow his older brother into the ministry; Blair Roberts, then an Episcopal priest, would

Trinity College track team, 1906. Paul Roberts is second from left in white robe. *Cathedral archives.*

eventually become the bishop of South Dakota. Paul Roberts graduated from Berkeley Divinity School in 1912, and the same year married Marion Legate of Newburyport, Massachusetts. Their wedding trip was spent bicycling through England, Wales, and Scotland, visiting the many cathedrals there.

Later that year Paul Roberts began a seven-year ministry at the mission churches at DeSmet and Brookings, South Dakota, where he also coached the South Dakota State College football team. In Brookings, St Paul's new church building was built during his tenure. It was in Brookings that his unwavering conviction as a pacifist and champion of the oppressed was first noted. In fact, during World War I, he was reported to the local sheriff for being disloyal to the country: he had supported a gentle, German-born florist who had been incarcerated despite his loyalty to his adopted country. As a result of this incident, Roberts published an article entitled "Who Were the Cowards?", which got him into further trouble! Roberts served briefly in West Orange, New Jersey, before being called as dean of St. Michael's Cathedral in Boise, Idaho, where he remained for seven years. He was elected rector of Grace and St. Stephen's Church, Colorado Springs, in 1928, and led that congregation through eight difficult years of the Great Depression.

It was now 1936, and Roberts became rector of Saint John's Church in the Wilderness and dean of St. John's Cathedral. In February, as dean-elect, Roberts wrote to the congregation:

> I am looking forward eagerly to my ministry among you. It is a very great tradition upon which we in St. John's Cathedral have to build. With all humility we must make that past the foundation for a still greater future. Every task well done finds its greatest meaning as the starting point for a new responsibility accepted. Our lives must have a continuity, but they must also be constantly refreshed by new beginnings.[85]

For many parishioners, especially those who had grown up during his tenure, Roberts will always be "The Dean." His intense commitment to his fellow persons took many forms. As a pacifist, he often said, "We must destroy war or it will destroy us." He championed the rights of minorities and women and is remembered for his early civil rights stands, long before most people had even thought to question their own comfortable positions in these areas. His stands on these issues kept him in hot water, even with his own congregation, for he had a way of pricking consciences and making the comfortable feel great discomfort. The local press referred to him as "the red dean." He wanted the support and backing of the Church in his fervent causes, but was realistic and had a light humorous touch, even in such serious matters. Once when someone suggested that Dean Roberts was unhappy with the Church, the dean told the story of a passenger who asked a streetcar conductor if he could not go faster. The conductor replied, "Yes, but I have to stay with the car"—and the dean had to stay with the Church.

Dean Roberts was a dynamic preacher who expressed his Christian theology in understandable terms and always added a large helping of humor.[86] He said that whether giving a talk or a sermon, "humor is the social lubricant, and a light touch gives a sense of perspective to whatever one has to say."[87] He was also known for his many stories, poems, and limericks.

Tragedy also played a role in his life as dean of St. John's. He had been dean about fifteen months when he suffered a great personal loss. Marion Roberts, driving their five children and their young friend, was hit head-on in a highway accident. Mrs. Roberts was seriously injured and three of their children less so. Two of their children, Anne Legate Roberts and Paul Roberts Jr., and the friend, Jeanne Quistgaard, were killed. Four days later Dean Roberts, together with his brother, Bishop Blair Roberts, and Bishops Johnson and Ingley, conducted the funeral service for the three young people in St. John's Cathedral. Mrs. Roberts was hospitalized and unable to attend the funeral, but later recovered.

Dean Roberts was a tireless leader. From the beginning, he initiated new programs and organizations to further the ministry of St. John's. He began publishing *The Open Door* in 1936, and organized a Parish Council and an Auxiliary Junior Vestry to broaden the role of laypeople. The Dean's Men not only served as a social group with weekly luncheons downtown and monthly dinners at the cathedral; they were the service group of the parish, painting the cathedral aisles, varnishing the floor, installing the new kneelers, tarring the roof, and more. Roberts created a Junior Auxiliary for the young women in the parish in the 1930s, and years later when these women were no longer young and the organization was renamed St. Martha's Guild, he began a new organization for the young women called St. Monica's Guild. These two groups added to the work of the Woman's Auxiliary, which also included the Evening Branch, the Daughters of the King, and the Christmas Sale or bazaar.[88] The bazaar involved dozens of parish members and nonmembers, women and men, some working year-round, to provide income to the church and more importantly, to provide a service to the people of the neighborhood.[89] The Mr. & Mrs. Club provided social activities for married couples of all ages. The youth activities included high school and junior high groups and the YAKs, young adult club, later called the YPF, young people's fellowship, and Boy Scouts, Camp Fire Girls, and the Girls Friendly Society.

In 1938 Roberts initiated what would become a longstanding relationship by adding Vine Deloria, a Sioux Indian priest in South Dakota, as missionary from St. John's.[90] During World War II there was a program to host young soldiers from nearby military camps as well as participation in the Canteen for the Armed Forces.

Another tradition started by the dean was called the "winding of the greens." Members of the congregation went to the mountains to cut Christmas trees and gather greens, and later met in the chapter house (and later in the education building) to wind wreaths and ropes to decorate the cathedral. This tradition continued beyond Dean Roberts' time until "made-by-hand" decorations were deemed not appropriate and were replaced by commercial decorations.

Dean Roberts inherited two assistants, Canon Watts and Canon Douglas. There was an amazing relationship between Paul Roberts and Harry Watts. They were very different in temperament and in churchmanship, yet they brought their diverse gifts together effectively for more than twenty years. The parish of St. John's was doubly blessed. In addition to Canon Watts and Canon Douglas, the dean hired a series of newly ordained clergy as assistants, so that the cathedral became a training ground for many successful priests.

The Reverend
Vine Deloria Sr.,
who served as
missionary from
the cathedral
from 1938 to 1951.
*Photo by Frank
Rowley, 1972.
Cathedral archives.*

Harry
Watts,
canon,
1925–1959.
*Cathedral
archives.*

Baptismal font from the first cathedral, installed in the northeast tower (baptistry) of the present cathedral in 1911. Rebuilt, lid added, and moved to the front of the nave in 1930 in memory of Milo A. and Henrietta E. Smith. In 1953, during removal of the Christmas decorations, a falling tree knocked over the font revealing a tin box with a list of the forty-eight children who had given the font in 1880. *Cathedral archives.*

Roberts also hired David Pew who, as organist and choirmaster, would lead the music program of the cathedral for thirty years. Pew inherited a mixed choir, and in September of 1940 he reported that the choir was now all-male with some fifty boys and several men participating. He recruited boys from many of the Denver Public Schools.[91] For the family service, there was also a girls' choir, which included as many as sixty-five girls. Pew was drafted during World War II and was absent from the cathedral for about fifteen months. He returned with Estelle, his new wife, and together they ran the music program. One of the highlights of the Christmas season was the dean's roller skating party at Mammoth Gardens for the choirs and Sunday School, and the Easter highlight for the boy's choir was lunch at the Denver Country Club hosted by Senator Lawrence C. Phipps.

The physical plant changed, too. In 1938, when it was apparent that the old organ wasn't going to last, Mrs. Lawrence C. Phipps gave a new Kimball or-

The primary department choir in St. Martin's Chapel, ca. 1940. On the far left of the second row is Paul Towner, now a retired priest; and on the left of the back row is Nancy Joyce, now a cathedral archivist. *Woodward collection.*

gan in memory of her father, Platt Rogers, former mayor of Denver. Fred H. Meunier of Denver, who installed the organ, wrote in 1973, "St. John's organ is a very fine, well-built instrument, containing qualities of materials and workmanship far superior to any that can be found in organs today."[92] During the late 1940s the choir area was renovated under the direction of Burnham Hoyt, the resident architect. Choir pews were replaced using the same end pieces, and new frontals, wainscot and canopy carvings were added, depicting the flora and fauna of the Rocky Mountains. The dean's stall and canon's stall were added.

David Raymond Pew, organist and choirmaster, 1939–1970, at the console
of the Platt Rogers Memorial Organ. He came to Denver from the Church
of the Advent, Cincinnati, retired in 1970, and that year was awarded a
doctor of music degree from Marietta College. *Cathedral archives.*

Thirteen of the clerestory windows in the cathedral were installed. The windows on the west and five of the windows on the east followed the revised plan
of 1935, but, in a third change, the last window was filled with more contemporary church figures, the "Modern Heroes" window, was given in part by Paul
and Marion Roberts.

Boys' choir, 1947. Note the four choir stalls rather than the present three. This picture was taken after the east wainscot and canopy were added (October 1946), but before the installation of the west wainscot and canopy, the dean's and canon's stalls, and the choir stall frontals (December 1948). *Photo by Floyd H. McCall. Cathedral archives.*

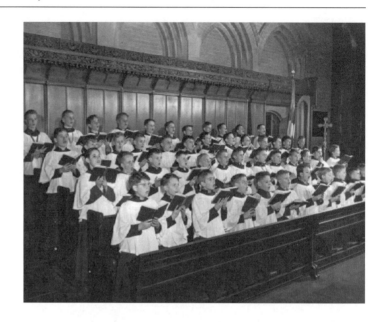

The girls' St. Cecelia Choir, 1947, outside St. Martin's Chapel. On the right is the south end of the chapter house. The three blank window areas held the center three stained-glass windows from the first cathedral from 1904 to 1911, when they were installed in the present cathedral. *Photo by Floyd H. McCall. Cathedral archives.*

Dean Roberts's roller skating party at Mammoth Gardens (now Fillmore auditorium) at Colfax Avenue and Clarkson Street, ca. 1945. *Cathedral archives.*

Easter and Christmas services became so crowded that tickets were issued for these services, and to get the Christmas message to a broader audience, the Christmas Eve service was broadcast on radio starting in 1941. By the 1950s, this service was broadcast on local television, a tradition that continued into the 1970s. In 1947 the dean ended a tradition that had been a part of St. John's for many years: parishioners could no longer rent pews for services. These pew rentals had been a principal source of income, so the emphasis was now shifted to the pledge. Old habits were hard to change, however, and as long as many "old timers" lived they sat in the same previously rented pew.

Seating habits were not the only things that were hard to change. In the apse, the old windows from the first cathedral had served well in the new cathedral for more than forty years, but by 1951 it had become apparent to the vestry that the combination of fire and age had taken its toll. Dean Roberts contacted the Connick Studios in Boston, who were working on the last clerestory

Carving from choir pew frontal. *Photo by Jim Nelson, 2000. Cathedral Archives.*

Dean Roberts observes the installation of the new organ pipes in 1938. Note absence of wainscoting and canopy on the east wall behind the choir pews. *Cathedral archives.*

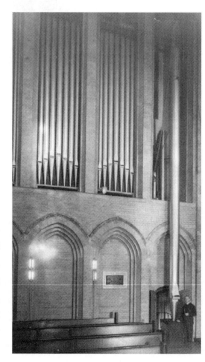

The old sacristy and hallway. Stairway from chancel leads down to what is now the Shannon Room. In 1950 the present sacristy was built over the south end of this room and the vestment case was moved to the new sacristy. *Cathedral archives.*

window, to design new windows for the apse. Replacing the old windows was not to be accomplished easily. Many members of the congregation objected strongly to replacing the old windows, and began writing letters to the dean, to the vestry and to the newspapers. One parishioner wrote to the vestry:

> The main point is this: can St. John's escape dishonor in accepting tens of thousands of dollars for specific memorials and then, at some later date, junk the memorials and palm off the donors with a perfunctory placque [*sic*] tacked around somewhere?[93]

The Right Reverend Harold L. Bowen, the new bishop coadjutor, in St. Martin's Chapel shortly after his consecration on September 29, 1947. Bowen was diocesan bishop 1949–1955. *Photo from The Living Church. Cathedral archives.*

Not all the letters voiced objections. Eleanor Hart Hanington wrote:

> My father, when Dean of our first Cathedral, brought over from England the finest stained glass in his opinion that was made at that time, and I think that now that these windows are in a very bad state of repair, he would want them replaced by the best glass obtainable now.[94]

Then the conflict moved to the streets. As the apocryphal story goes, somehow an enraged parishioner and prominent historical writer took the cartoons [window designs] and fled with them in her car. Hot on her trail, Dean Roberts followed her home and eventually convinced her to return the cartoons. Soon the

Dean Roberts in the office of Mayor J. Quigg Newton Jr., February 1948, on the occasion of the establishment of the Mayor's Survey Committee on Human Relations, to be headed by Dean Roberts. *Photo by Syd Joseph. Cathedral archives.*

vestry offered a compromise: the three center windows would remain, and the four outside windows would be replaced with Connick windows. One month after Dean Roberts retired in 1957, the issue resolved itself when a windstorm blew out a significant portion of one of the center windows. All of the windows would be replaced.

The dean was also a builder of missions. In 1947 a mission was established in Lakewood called St. Paul's Church, which met in a Quonset hut. Canon Gerrit Barnes of the cathedral became its first vicar, followed by Canon Ainsley Carlton, who led the mission for two years. In 1951 a new church building, designed by cathedral architect James Sudler, was built. By early 1952 St. John's Mission was established in southeast Denver, meeting first in Kent School, until a new building was built in 1954. This mission became Christ Church in 1956, and Canon Gerrit Barnes of the cathedral, the mission's vicar,

St. Paul's Church, Lakewood, at 10th and Garrison streets. Organized in 1947, building in 1951. *Photo by Dave Allinger. Cathedral archives.*

Christ Church, 2460 E. Bates. Organized in 1952, building in 1954. *Photo by Louise Pote. Cathedral archives.*

St. Philip and St. James Church, 2797 So. Lowell Blvd. Organized in 1955, building in 1958. *Cathedral archives.*

In the dean's study, ca. 1954. Canons Vernon Myers and Harry Watts stand behind Dean Paul Roberts. *Cathedral archives.*

became its first rector. The pattern was to repeat itself in 1955 when the cathedral established the mission of St. Philip and St. James in southwest Denver, which met in temporary quarters, until a new building was built in 1958. Canon Vernon Myers was instrumental in the development of this mission and became its vicar and then its first rector when it became a parish several years later. He served St. Philip and St. James until his retirement in 1987.

The years 1954 to 1957 were a time of significant optimism and participation at St. John's. The Korean War had ended, Eisenhower was president, baby boomers were everywhere, and going to church was "in." And while many churches were moving to the suburbs, the building of a new education and music building was a clear sign that St. John's was committed to the inner city. Dean Roberts reported in February of 1957:

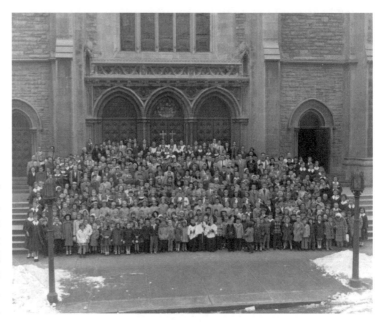

St. John's Sunday School, ca. 1954. Canon Vernon Myers is in front of the righthand pier next to the open door. *Cathedral archives.*

> One does not reckon the success or failure of the Church in terms of numbers, but it is often an indication of interest and concern. At any rate here are a few. For the first time our number of communicants has passed the three thousand mark and our Church School, if the Dean's Bible Class is included, numbers over one thousand.[95]

When Roberts had arrived in 1936, there were fourteen hundred members and a Sunday School of fifty-five. Now both the parish house and the chapter house were overcrowded. The main portion of the chapter house was a gymnasium with classrooms ringing the balcony. The fifty-year-old building was in bad repair, and rather than try to fix it up, it was decided to build a thirty-thousand square-foot building on the site of the old ten-thousand square-foot chapter house. So down it came.

The north end
of the chapter
house, ca. 1954.
The main room
has become
a gymnasium
with open Sunday
School rooms
on the balcony.
(See similar view
on page 48).
Cathedral archives.

Ground was broken in August of 1955 for the new education and music
building. The architects were Fisher, Fisher and Davis; Burnham Hoyt was consulting architect and the general contractor was Gerald Phipps, Inc. Many Sunday School classes were held in Morey Junior High during construction. The
Sunday School occupied the new building in September of 1956, the first bazaar
held in the new building was in November, and dedication was on February 21,
1957. Unknown to Dean Roberts, the vestry had decided to name the building
for him. He was surprised at the dedication when Bishop Minnis said, "From
now on, the building will be known as the Dean Paul Roberts Building—and
that is praise he can never escape."[96]

When Paul Roberts retired on Easter of 1957 after twenty-one years as
dean, the whole city joined in honoring him. Roscoe Fleming wrote in the *Denver Post*: "If he does not retire as Denver's first citizen, name me one who better

Surveying the result of razing the chapter house to clear the site for the Roberts building in 1955. Only the smoke stack and about fifteen feet of the cloister remained. *Cathedral archives.*

Ground breaking for the new education and music building in August, 1955. Left to right: David Pew (at organ), Bishop Joseph Minnis (behind Pew), Canon Harry Watts, Canon Vern Myers, and Dean Paul Roberts. In background is 1950 clergy sacristy. *Cathedral archives.*

Sexton's house, razed May 1957, sited approximately in the present parking lot. *Cathedral archives.*

Crossing Clarkson Street to Morey Junior High School for Sunday School classes following the 9:30 A.M. family service, ca. 1955. *Cathedral archives.*

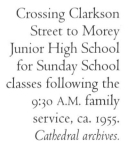

The new education and music building under construction in
1956. (Clarkson Street is just to left of trees bordering sidewalk.)
It was named the Dean Paul Roberts Building in February 1957.
Cathedral archives.

deserves the designation."[97] And Dr. Allen Breck wrote, "He was not merely the
dean of a cathedral, he was a dean of humanity."[98] He was honored by the
Colorado branch of the American Civil Liberties Union and at a citywide reception at the University of Denver. The National Jewish Foundation honored
him at the BMH Congregation with a tribute by Rabbi Emeritus Charles E. H.
Kauvar. He was cited as "Lover of God—Champion of Every Good Cause—
Pursuer of Righteousness—Seeker of Peace—Friend of Man."[99] An admirer
said, "He carved a reputation as the father of the human rights-civil rights

Dean Roberts at his
retirement in 1957.
His wife, Marion,
wrote, "This is you.
Taken on the last day.
You would insist on
wearing that hat!"
Cathedral archives.

movement in Denver."[100] And Mayor Tom Currigan, presenting him the
Mayor's Award for Public Service a few years earlier, cited him for "his work as a
pioneer in Denver's struggle for human rights during an era when it was far less
popular than it is today. Denver would not have achieved what it has today if it
were not for Dean Roberts."[101]

　　　　Dean Roberts' retirement did not mean rest. He referred to himself as
"retread, not retired." He immediately served several months as dean of the
cathedral in Honolulu, and the next year served as interim dean of Trinity Cathedral in Phoenix. Paul and Marion Roberts bought a home in Phoenix, spending their winters there and summers at their home on Cape Cod. At this time he
began to create the lovely stained glass medallions, many of which are still

Paul Roberts, "The Dean of Humanity." *Photo by Lainson Studio. Cathedral archives.*

displayed at the cathedral. Marion Roberts died in 1980 and the dean in 1984. His life is best reflected by the prayer he said before each sermon:

> Lord, keep our hearts sound, Our lives brave, Our thinking straight, And our spirits humble; That we may be true interpreters of Thy life to our fellowmen.

Marion and Paul Roberts at Wellfleet, Cape Cod, Massachusetts, 1966.
Cathedral archives.

7. Dean Lea, 1958–1962

ALTHOUGH DEAN ROBERTS HAD INTENDED TO RETIRE January 1, 1957, he stayed until Easter because the vestry had a difficult time finding a new dean. Two priests refused the position, and the Reverend Harry Watts, the incredible, faithful canon, was appointed priest-in-charge until the Reverend William Sentelle Lea accepted the call.

Dr. Lea, his wife, Jean, and their two daughters arrived in Denver in the first week of September 1957; he became rector of Saint John's Church in the Wilderness on September 8, and was installed dean of St. John's Cathedral on October 10, 1957, by Bishop Minnis. Born in Easton, Washington, William Lea was ordained in 1935 and earned a doctor of divinity degree from the University of the South in Sewanee, Tennessee, eighteen years later. At the time he was called to St. John's, he was the editor of *The Episcopal Church News* and an associate editor of *The Living Church.* He was a well-known theologian and author of relig-

Dr. William Sentelle
Lea, fifth dean of
St. John's Cathedral,
1957–1962.
Cathedral archives.

ious publications. Dean Lea was a preacher much in demand, a significant factor because he had had polio, which left his vocal cords impaired. He had been told that he would not talk again, but his voice was fully restored. His involvement in national and international church affairs took him away from the cathedral a great deal, and some parishioners objected to his traveling so much. He had a very effective ministry with some portions of the cathedral congregation, but lacked the common touch that had endeared Dean Roberts to the parish.

Unlike Dean Roberts, Lea hired experienced priests as canons who could take responsibilities for portions of the church's ministry, such as Christian social relations, parish visitations, and youth work, thus assuring that the programs in these areas would continue during his many absences. Dean Lea hired four assistants[102] during his brief stay in Denver, and two of them played significant roles at St. John's for many years. In 1958 he hired the Reverend Russell Kaoru Nakata, who was born in Pennsylvania to Japanese immigrant parents who had moved from Honolulu to Pennsylvania, and finally to California, where he grew up. He graduated from McCormick Theological Seminary, Chicago, and for five years was a minister in the Presbyterian Church, his first job being chaplain in a relocation center for Japanese-Americans during World War II. He was later ordained in the Episcopal Church and was curate of the Church of the Ascension in Chicago before coming to the cathedral. Canon Nakata was hired to be responsible for Christian social relations and for community service.

The next year Dean Lea hired Herbert Monroe Barrall, another native Pennsylvanian, who was a graduate of Virginia Theological Seminary. He had been a curate in Connecticut, a rector in Ohio, and rector of Grace Church, Middletown, New York, before coming to Denver in June 1959. Hired to share the pastoral responsibilities with the dean, Herbert Barrall, his wife, Grace, and their three children arrived in Denver in 1959.

Dean Lea's time as dean of the cathedral was marked by several problems. First, it was impossible to fill the shoes of Dean Roberts. Many parishioners could not accept what they considered to be less than "The Dean." In addition, Lea simply could not get along with Bishop Minnis, who had been consecrated two years before Lea's arrival, nor could the bishop get along with the dean.

But perhaps more important were his difficulties when it came to finances. The vestry minutes indicate that in addition to the burdensome cost of his extensive travels, he was inclined to make expenditures of significant amounts without consulting with the vestry. Some felt that the vestry seemed to condone his actions, which led to what has been called "the revolution," an

In the new library, ca. 1959. Standing left to right: Dean Lea, Canon Ravenel, and Canon Nakata. Seated: Bishop Minnis and Helen Arndt. *Cathedral archives.*

event that significantly changed the way the parish elects members of the vestry. At that time it was customary for the dean and a small committee to nominate a single slate to be elected at the annual meeting. This meeting was held in the parish hall, so that about 200 to 250 parishioners elected the vestry. In 1961 it was felt that the "dean's slate" would continue to condone the financial expenditures. Initially the meeting seemed to be quite normal, but following dinner more parishioners crowded into the parish hall in time for the election. When the outgoing senior warden went through what was normally only a customary procedure of asking for nominations from the floor, things began to happen. In quick succession, nominations and seconds for the openings of junior warden and three vestry members were made, followed by a motion to close the nominations. Those nominated from the floor were elected by nearly identical counts. The outgoing senior warden and the dean were speechless.

In his report at the next vestry meeting, the dean tried to cope with the situation saying, "That there was a rebellion is obvious, but doesn't this show a deep concern? And shouldn't we interpret this in a positive way?" He also quoted Thomas Jefferson saying, "I hold it, that a little rebellion now and then is a good thing." However, the minutes indicate that from that time on the vestry clamped down on his expenditures, and that there was much tension between the dean and the vestry. The dean continued in office, saying that he had no intention of not being the dean, but, by December, he had received a call to another church and presented his letter of resignation to the vestry.

In January of 1962, Dr. Lea was installed as rector of Christ Church in Winnetka, Illinois, on Chicago's North Shore, then the second largest church in the diocese of Chicago and called one of the "most important churches in the Midwest."[103] In a letter to Louisa Arps, the cathedral archivist, a few years later, he describes this church: "We are indeed happy here. . . . This is, as you perhaps know, a very affluent community and represents what we facetiously call the 'power structure.'"[104] Lea stayed at Christ Church until he retired in 1977. During this time he was called to be dean of another cathedral, but refused the call. Dean Lea died in 1984.

8. *The Barrall Years: Times of Change, 1963–1980*

FOLLOWING DEAN LEA'S DEPARTURE, THE VESTRY intended to name Canon Barrall as interim rector and dean in December of 1961; however, the bishop indicated that this "would automatically remove him as a candidate for the [permanent] Deanship." To avoid the situation that the vestry thought unfair to Barrall, they decided to ask recently retired Bishop Dagwell to return to St. John's as interim rector, it being understood, tacitly, that Canon Barrall would continue to supervise the total work of the clergy in the parish. And so, twenty-six years after leaving to become the bishop of Oregon, Benjamin Dagwell returned to St. John's for a period of three months.

Benjamin Dagwell,
retired bishop
of Oregon and
"the Bishop's Vicar"
of St. John's, 1962.
Cathedral archives.

After returning to Oregon, Bishop Dagwell wrote to Canon Barrall in June 1962, urging him to stay at the cathedral, "You are a beacon of light, an anchor, a workhorse and several other things that a Parish Priest and a man of God should be. Seldom are so many qualities found in one man."[105]

For the next ten months, Canon Barrall ran the cathedral "without title." Through the Roberts years, the evangelical (low) church services did not regularly include eucharistic vestments; in fact the cathedral owned only one gold set for Easter and Christmas and borrowed others as needed from St. Luke's Hospital. However, such vestments had begun to be used on a more frequent basis in the Church generally by this time. At the vestry meeting on

At the installation of Herbert M. Barrall as rector of Saint John's Church in the Wilderness, February 10, 1963. Clergy, left to right: Canon Nakata, Bishop Minnis, Barrall, and Canon Gresham. Others are members of the vestries of 1962 and 1963. *Photo by L. A. Lucas. Cathedral archives.*

November 29, 1962, the senior warden reported word from the bishop that the cathedral should purchase its own eucharistic vestments. Change was coming.

Canon Herbert Monroe Barrall was elected rector of Saint John's Church in the Wilderness on February 10, 1963. Even though there had been attempts to reconcile the problems with the bishop and diocese, Bishop Minnis insisted that although the parish elected its rector, the bishop appointed the dean, and he refused to do so at this time. Seven months later he wrote the vestry:

> I have decided to install the Reverend Herbert M. Barrall, rector of St. John's Church, as dean at the eleven o'clock service on September 29, 1963, at a joint service of all the parishes and missions in the diocese, starting the tenth year of my Episcopate.[106]

Herbert Barrall, the new rector receives congratulations from former seminary classmate, February 10, 1963. Left to right: the Reverend and Mrs. John C. Mott, Mark Barrall, Herbert Barrall, Grace Barrall, Sara Barrall, and Ann Terry Barrall. *Photo by L. A. Lucas. Cathedral archives.*

The new dean was aware of "the revolution" of 1961. In what appeared to be an attempt to ensure that it would not happen again, he instituted the nomination of multiple candidates for each vestry office and the mail-in ballot. These are still in use, enabling all parishioners to participate in the election.

Dean Barrall set about expanding what he called the "team ministry." Following Dean Lea's example, he hired experienced priests to share in the ministry of St. John's Cathedral. In June of 1964, Dean Barrall hired the Reverend Frank Rowley, a West Virginia native and graduate of Virginia Theological Seminary, where they had been friends. Frank Rowley, his wife, Bonnie, and their three children came to Denver from Bluefield, West Virginia. Rowley had

Herbert Monroe Barrall, the tenth rector of Saint John's Church in the Wilderness and the sixth dean of St. John's Cathedral. *Cathedral archives.*

been involved with activities of the national Church and with numerous summer conferences. He was hired to concentrate on pastoral work, youth work, and stewardship. In his fifteen years at St. John's, he was particularly effective as pastor to the congregation, a very warm and understanding priest who had a homey touch. He was frequently at the piano, playing the old favorites for the enjoyment of all, especially the senior citizens, and he was frequently tapped to "call" square dances in the parish hall. Canon Rowley was producer and master of ceremonies for the television program "House of the Lord" presented by the Colorado Council of Churches. Under his direction the Choir Camp became the Cathedral Youth Camp, open to all young members of the congregation. Canon Rowley and his Polaroid camera were everywhere recording the life of St. John's on film.

Services at
Gold Lake
Camp, 1968,
led by
Canon Wells.
*Cathedral
archives.*

A year after the arrival of Frank Rowley, another experienced priest was added to the staff, the Reverend Llewellyn W. Wells, another West Virginian and graduate of Virginia Theological Seminary. Lew Wells, his wife, Marge, and their three children came to Denver from Kanawha City, West Virginia. At St. John's, Wells was in charge of Christian education and the youth work of the parish. His first duty on arrival in Colorado was to drive to Woodland Park, west of Colorado Springs, where the St. John's camp was in session. Under his direction the camping program of the cathedral moved from Thunderbird Camp in Woodland Park to Gold Lake Camp near Ward, then to Gold Hill above Boulder, and finally to Geneva Glen Camp at Indian Hills. He was effective with the youth group during the very difficult time for young people—the 1960s.

Canon Nakata continued at St. John's. During the twenty-four years he was canon of the cathedral, his most significant contribution was his work on

The "team ministry," ca. 1973. Left to right: Canon Frank Rowley, Canon Russell Nakata, Dean Herbert Barrall, and Canon Llewellyn Wells. *Photo by William Rice Jr. Cathedral archives.*

the Cathedral Social Services Committee, taking the responsibility for the diocesan ministry. At the time of Nakata's retirement in 1983, the Episcopal Pastoral Center was giving emergency aid to over nine hundred individuals a week. Outside the cathedral, Canon Nakata is best known for his work with housing for Denver's poor and aging. Appointed by Mayor William McNichols, he served on the Denver Housing Authority for fourteen years, nine years as its chair.

By 1965 the "team ministry" was in place, and the next several years were a time of growth and a high level of activity. In 1966 the average attendance at all Sunday services reached the highest ever recorded, over eleven hundred.[107] In addition to the many parish functions, the cathedral provided space for two weekday schools, the Denver Cooperative Nursery School and the Denver Board School for the Mentally Retarded and Seriously Handicapped. The Colorado Council of Churches also moved into the cathedral facilities.

David Raymond Pew, after his retirement as Cathedral organist and choirmaster in 1970. Dr. Pew died in Wichita, Kansas, in 2000. *Photo by Berkeley-Lainson. Cathedral archives.*

In the music department, Dr. Pew retired as organist and choirmaster and was replaced by Robert Finster. He had earned his degree of doctor of musical arts from Eastman School of Music, and had been organist and choirmaster of Grace Episcopal Church in Elmira, New York and director of music at Twelve Corners Presbyterian Church in Rochester, New York. Dr. Finster began an ambitious music program, calling it "Music/St. John's." He created a new concert choir called "Cathedral Singers," which was wonderfully received. Following a concert given by the Cathedral Singers in Evergreen, the *Canyon Courier* reported:

> Those who are concerned, amidst rapid changes and startling innovations, will be happy to know that Church Music is alive and well, and

Dr. Robert
Finster, organist
and choirmaster,
1970–1976.
Cathedral archives.

living in Colorado. Conducted by Dr. Robert Finster, the Cathedral Singers of St. John's Cathedral in Denver is an ecumenical group of volunteer singers of various religious and cultural backgrounds, who blend their voices together because they still love and embrace the great sacred music of all the ages.[108]

The *Denver Post* music critic wrote:

Sunday afternoons have been considerably enlivened thanks to a series called "Music/St. John's" which sums up the idea nicely in its title. The place is St. John's Episcopal Cathedral and the purpose is music, whether by the Cathedral Singers, the resident ensemble, or by guests. . . . Since its opening, Music/St. John's has become a major force in the city's musical life.[109]

These free concerts were attended by standing-room-only crowds.

In spite of the growth at the cathedral, the 1960s marked the beginning of a time when both local and national events would create disturbance and turmoil in the life of the parish. By 1965, the Civil Rights movement had begun. That year Canon Nakata and a cathedral parishioner, Dr. Karl Arndt, joined the Civil Rights March from Selma to Montgomery. In a few years this movement would lead to the desegregation of the Denver Public Schools and the "white flight to the suburbs." Dean Barrall and the cathedral were about to go through that difficult time called "change." There was confusion about the cathedral's role in the desegregation of the schools. The youth group's activities supporting Civil Rights and environmental efforts and opposing the Vietnam War offended some of the cathedral members. Historically St. John's, and specifically its clergy, had been a positive influence on the life of Denver, but during these times, St. John's seemed to express a wavering stance about most of these issues.

A 1968 event seemed to mark the end of the good times of Dean Barrall's years at the cathedral. Bishop Minnis had been criticized for financial transactions that some felt were unnecessary or inappropriate: building of a new Diocesan Center apart from the cathedral, the purchase of Trinity Ranch, and the acquisition of a new bishop's residence. But the bishop's troubles were compounded by charges of inappropriate behavior. The result was that an ecclesiastical court of nine bishops was convened in Dagwell Hall at St. John's. The *Rocky Mountain News* reported, "Bishop Minnis has been charged by 17 clergy and lay members of the Colorado diocese with breach of his ordination vows. The specific charges involve personal conduct."[110] At this time Bishop Minnis was a patient in a Colorado Springs hospital, and his doctor stated that he was not able to stand trial because of a heart condition. The trial never got underway, and the court recessed after Minnis was ordered to relinquish his authority as bishop immediately and to leave the diocese of Colorado. Not surprisingly, the local and national press took full advantage of this tragic situation.

The trial of Bishop Minnis in Dagwell Hall on September 24, 1968.
Photo by Frank Rowley. Cathedral archives.

But the trial had also taken its toll on Dean Barrall, who had been thrust into the leadership role, and on many others who had taken part in the action against the bishop. The dean and several of the others now were encouraged to become candidates for bishop. However, this was not to be, and Suffragan Bishop Edward Thayer was elected diocesan bishop in 1969.

With the advent of the 1970s, times were then complicated by the approved ordination of women and by the movement to revise the *Book of Common Prayer* and the consequent introduction of trial liturgies. These events had an unsettling effect on the congregation at St. John's. Many parishioners felt that the trial liturgies were simply a "tryouts," and that by signing petitions against them, they would be withdrawn. Dean Barrall tried to alleviate the bad feelings

Planning for the future at the cathedral, 1969. Seated left to right: Canon Wells, Canon Rowley, and Dean Barrall. Standing: Jane Bowes (Mrs. Eugene), coordinator of the Cathedral Development Planning Commission; Canon Nakata, and Dr. R. T. Lyford, parish visitor. *Cathedral archives.*

by emphasizing the "trial" aspect of the new services, but changes to the liturgy were mandated by the national Church. For many, these changes were nothing short of an ordeal, which would result in more change, even in staunch parishioners leaving St. John's or the Episcopal Church altogether. In 1979, the National Episcopal Convention would again meet in Denver, and on the agenda was the adoption of the new prayer book.[III]

Christmas Eve, 1974. Clergy left to right: Dean Barrall, canons Nakata (celebrant) and Rowley. Note freestanding altar on temporary platform at foot of stairs from chancel. Pews at front of nave and one row of choir stalls had not yet been removed. *Photo by Thomas Rowley. Cathedral archives.*

During the 1970s average attendance at St. John's services fell to disastrous levels, fewer than five hundred.[112] Membership fell and Sunday School attendance dropped below one hundred. Several parish leadership conferences were held to try to revive the congregation. At the beginning of this period, the new bishop, William Frey, attempted to start a charismatic renewal movement at the cathedral; but this movement touched only a few members and after five years there was only a slight increase in attendance. In a letter to the members of

The Capital Hill People's Fair was held at St. John's and Morey Middle School on May 10, 1975. Note that Clarkson Street was closed for fair activities. *Photo by Jim Manson. Cathedral archives.*

Clergy and lay members gather on the front steps of the cathedral after it was added to the National Register of Historic Places in August 1975. The cathedral had been designated a Denver Landmark in April 1968. *Cathedral archives.*

The Right
Reverend William
Carl Frey and
Barbara Frey.
Frey was bishop
of Colorado from
1973 to 1990.
Cathedral archives.

the congregation dated December 26, 1979, the dean wrote: "Holy Scripture tells us 'For every thing there is a time.' After much thought and prayer, I believe the time has come for me to take the necessary steps to relinquish my position as Dean of St. John's Cathedral."[113] The resignation, which was to take place no later than June of 1980, was made by mutual agreement with the vestry.

Herb Barrall had been at the cathedral for twenty-one years, seventeen as dean. In reviewing his accomplishments as dean at the request of the vestry, he included: "Welcomed the first black member of the cathedral vestry (Jim Burress), the first woman from this parish to become a member of the vestry (Elizabeth Brown), the first young (under age 30) person to become a member

Kate
Knapp,
assisting
deacon,
1979,
administering
the chalice
in the
cathedral.
Courtesy,
Colorado
Episcoplian.

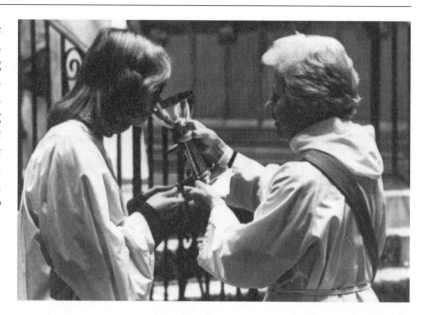

Construction
of All Souls'
Walk, 1966.
Looking
south
from 14th
Avenue.
Cathedral
archives.

Future site of
Cathedral Square
North from the
cathedral steps,
April 1978.
Cathedral archives.

of our vestry (Marquis Bell), and the first ordained woman to become a part of
our clergy staff (Kate Knapp)."[114] Improvements in the facilities included the
creation of All Souls' Walk columbarium, and the land acquisition for the development of Cathedral Square North. The return of the diocesan offices to the
cathedral grounds, a joint effort of the dean and Bishop Frey, resulted in the
new Diocesan Center. The cathedral stonework and lighting underwent major
repair and renovation, and new windows were installed above the altar and organ
console. The dean's office became the Common Room. With money left by
Bishop Dagwell after his death, the parish house was renovated including the installation of an elevator and the plumbing on the third floor, and the building
and parish hall were named for him. There were several new innovations in the
services, including the "Kirkin' o' the Tartan" and the use of balloons at Easter.
The list of accomplishments is extensive, but the truth was that these were difficult times, and by 1980 the former vitality of St. John's was depleted.

Approaching
the cathedral from
the newly completed
Cathedral Square
North, 1979. *Courtesy,
Colorado Episcopalian.*

Scaffolding for
window repair and
stone pointing in
1969. *Photo by Frank
Rowley. Cathedral
archives.*

Parish house from 13th Avenue, September, 1963, prior to the elevator tower. *Cathedral archives.*

Parish house from 13th Avenue, July 1964, after adding the elevator tower. *Cathedral archives.*

The "team ministry" underwent many changes following Barrall's resignation. On July 1 of 1980, Canon Russell Nakata was appointed priest-in-charge of St. John's Cathedral and the vestry turned their attention to finding a new dean. Canon Nakata stayed on the staff until April of 1983, serving under a third dean. Appointed honorary clergy associate in 1983, and canon emeritus in 1989, Russell Nakata continued his tireless efforts in the greater Denver community. He died in 1996. Frank Rowley retired in 1979 and was an honorary canon until his death in 1982. Canon Wells resigned in 1977, served churches in Breckenridge and Leadville and as chaplain at St. Anne's School and Spalding Rehabilitation Hospital. He is now retired and enjoying his grandchildren. In July of 1980, Herb Barrall was called to be rector of St. Mark's Episcopal Church in Barrington Hills, Illinois, where he served for several years. Upon his retirement, the Barralls moved to Salem, Oregon, where they are near their children and grandchildren.

Easter morning at St. John's Cathedral. Balloons have been a tradition since the mid-1970s. *Cathedral archives.*

9. *The McPhail Years: More Change and Growth, 1981–1990*

—————◆◇◆—————

THE SELECTION OF THE NEXT DEAN OF ST. JOHN'S CATHEDRAL was conducted quite differently from those of previous times. More than a hundred candidates were screened by the selection committee, and after visits to many of them, six were invited to Denver to preach and meet the congregation. Although some felt that the process became a popularity contest, it allowed the congregation to become really involved with the election for the first time. On December 7, 1980, the vestry announced the selection of Donald Stewart McPhail as the next dean of St. John's Cathedral. They had chosen a "take charge" kind of priest, a man with much charisma to lead the parish out of what appeared to be its lowest point.

A Montreal native, McPhail had had no religious upbringing and was occupied in the business world in Canada for six years. Quite by accident he became associated with the Anglican Church there and was later confirmed. Following graduation from Concordia University, he pursued further studies at the College of the Resurrection in Mirfield, Yorkshire, England, where he was certified for ordination by the Church of England, and through studies at General Theological Seminary in New York he earned a master of divinity degree. After ordination, he served briefly at the Lower East Side Mission of Trinity Church in New York. In 1963, he became curate of St. Peter's Church in Bay Shore, New York, becoming rector eight years later when the previous rector suddenly died. McPhail was a very successful rector of the Bay Shore parish, of approximately sixteen hundred members, with special emphasis on programs of evangelism, education, and music. He developed the reputation of being a "workaholic." There was so much going on that St. Peter's was dubbed "St. Activist's."

McPhail hesitated accepting the deanship in Denver. Recalling this time later, he indicated that he knew it was an enormous challenge, because he had been told that the cathedral was dispirited. He accepted the call with much trepidation, and his family experienced great sadness in leaving their familiar home and parish, but he said at the time that he was "filled with an overwhelming sense that this was the right thing to do."[115] With their three children, Donald and Randy McPhail arrived in Denver in the spring of 1981. He was instituted rector of Saint John's Church in the Wilderness and installed dean of St. John's Cathedral by Bishop William Frey on March 22. In his sermon the bishop said, "The work of selection of a dean for this cathedral started with prayer and continued with prayer. You are the answer to our prayers."[116]

Good and exciting things began to happen immediately. Within a year, attendance had increased fifty percent. Although the cathedral had a long history of outstanding music programs, this area had deteriorated following the

The installation of Donald McPhail as dean of the cathedral, March 22, 1981.
Left to right: Bishop William Frey, Bishop William Wolfrum, Donald McPhail,
the Reverend Robert Stiefel, and Canon Bruce Ravenel. *Cathedral archives.*

resignation of Dr. Finster in 1976. On September 1, 1981, McPhail hired Donald
Pearson, a young, energetic organist and choirmaster, and a wonderful revival of
the music programs of the cathedral was underway. Pearson studied at the
University of Wisconsin, Southern Methodist University, and the College-
Conservatory of Music in Cincinnati. He came to St. John's from Christ
Church, Glendale, Ohio, where he had been organist-choirmaster. He set about

Don Pearson, organist
and choir director. *Photo
by Thomas M. Rowley,
1985. Cathedral archives.*

improving the children's choir and augmenting the concert series. He began the
Friends of Music (a music support group), and launched Music with Lunch as
the first of several new programs. The *Denver Post* reported:

> Six months ago Donald Pearson got the job of organist-choirmaster
> at St. John's Episcopal Cathedral. Call him the Cincinnati cyclone, be-
> cause in just those six months he's become a one-man whirlwind of
> change and expansion in the musical affairs of the cathedral.[117]

To ensure the success of the many renewed programs of the cathedral,
Dean McPhail hired several new assistants,[118] among them the Reverend Robert

An important event happened at St. John's Cathedral on May 2, 1981. The Reverend Kathleen "Kay" Ryan was ordained the first woman priest in the diocese of Colorado. In 1970, Kay had been the first woman ordained deacon in the Episcopal Church. Left to right: Deacon Elizabeth Noice, Bishop William Frey, Kathleen Ryan, and Bishop William Wolfrum. *Woodward collection.*

J. (Rob) O'Neill, who was added as the new deacon of the cathedral in July 1981. A native of Pasadena, California, O'Neill was a magna cum laude graduate of Texas Christian University, and he held a master of divinity degree from Berkeley Divinity School, Yale University. Canon O'Neill was hired with primary responsibility for youth groups, children's worship, youth camps, and all work with boys and girls ages six to sixteen. A man of many talents, he was an accomplished jazz pianist, a published songwriter, a student of physics and American literature in college, a pretty good athlete, and a licensed pilot. He was ordained priest in January 1982. After ten years as canon at St. John's, O'Neill, with his wife, Ginger, and three children, moved to the Boston suburb of Winchester where he became rector of the Parish of the Epiphany in July 1991.

At the same service in January 1982, another new deacon was ordained, although David Forbes Morgan was not new to the cathedral. With his wife, Delores, he had been confirmed at St. John's in June of 1974. Before that he had been a minister of the Plymouth Brethren Church in his native Toronto in 1957. He was at one time president of the College of the Rockies in Golden, where he received his master of divinity degree. On November, 26, 1982, Wes French of the *Rocky Mountain News* wrote:

> A member of the Plymouth Brethren in Canada, a president of an evangelical Protestant college, a man interested in the possibility of becoming a Roman Catholic priest or monk, an ordained Episcopal priest. No, these aren't four different people. They are one man— David Forbes Morgan, who was ordained to the priesthood of the Episcopal Church in rites Monday night at St. John's Episcopal Cathedral in Denver.[119]

Inspired by a visit to an ecumenical community at Taizé, France, he started the Order of Christ-Centered Ministries in Denver in 1973 and became the prior of the order. During his fourteen years as canon of St. John's, he was a particularly effective pastoral minister, conducting funerals, ministering to the bereaved, comforting the sick, and taking the sacraments to the confined. In January of 1996 he retired as canon pastor of the cathedral to give himself more fully to the leadership of the order, and was named canon-at-large.

Perhaps the most significant changes in the life of St. John's during the 1980s had to do with the conduct of the worship services. Since its beginning in 1860, St. John's had been known as an evangelical or "low" church. This tradition had begun to change following the approval of the new prayer book in 1979.

Now, under the direction of McPhail, the services were filled with vestments, musical chants, incense ("bells and smells") and much of the pomp and pageantry that was once associated with a "high" church. This was an apparently welcome change that attracted many new attendees to the cathedral.

A very special service occurred in June of 1982. Her Royal Highness, The Princess Anne worshipped at the 9:00 A.M. service. The first twelve pews were reserved for dignitaries, the balance of the nave being seated on a first-come, first-served basis. But everyone had to be in place by 8:45 because all the doors were to be locked at that time. This author, as head usher at the event, later described the scene:

> Our job began long before the service. We had twenty-three ushers, four bomb-sniffing dogs, and innumerable police officers and various members of the Secret Service and Scotland Yard. This was the only time that the building was searched with dogs before the service. Across the street were demonstrators representing the Irish Republic faction. As the Sunday School children were gathered to greet Princess Anne, one usher asked a policeman who would protect the children if there was any violence. We were told that the police, Secret Service, and Scotland Yard were there to protect the Princess—it was up to us to protect the children. Fortunately there was no problem. We (the ushers) were glad when her limousine drove away![120]

Dean McPhail later said, "The *Denver Post* quoted some wag in saying it was 'an ordinary service.' You know it wasn't—in fact, it was an extraordinary service."[121]

Under McPhail's direction, the cathedral took on a new responsibility. A headline in the *Rocky Mountain News* on October 20, 1986 proclaimed, "Historic parish finds new identity as urban mission."[122] St. Andrew's, started by St. John's Sunday School in 1874, and thus the second oldest Episcopal church in Denver,

The visit of H.R.H., The Princess Anne, June 20, 1982. Left to right: Dean McPhail, Amy McPhail, and Princess Anne. *Cathedral archives.*

had just become a parochial mission of St. John's. Originally named Trinity Memorial Chapel, its parish membership had dropped to twelve, the building had become dilapidated, and its future looked bleak. The *News* continued:

> The wall above the altar of St. Andrew's Episcopal Church is covered with an ornate tempera and gold-leaf painting that includes, among its New Testament scenes, an image of St. John's Episcopal Cathedral. The cathedral's presence above the altar was especially fitting yesterday, when the dozen remaining members of St. Andrew's gathered for Mass, then voted to become a mission owned and operated by St. John's. The cathedral gave the painting to the historic downtown parish more than six decades ago.[123]

St. Andrew's Church (formerly Trinity Memorial Chapel), built at
20th and Glenarm streets in 1908, became the mission of St. John's
Cathedral in 1986. Designed by Ralph Adams Cram of Boston, the
building was never finished. *Cathedral archives.*

In 1985 Saint John's Church in the Wilderness celebrated its 125th anniversary. In its Michaelmas A.D. 1985 issue, the *Anglican Digest* featured the cathedral and wrote of "A Spirit-filled Church" and the success of its dean,
Donald McPhail:

> Today, over sixty groups vie for slots on the parish calendar, In the
> past four years the active Sunday congregation has increased from 500
> to 1,000 and the paid staff from 13 to 22 full-time employees. A few

125th anniversary celebrating the arrival of Father Kehler and family by stagecoach. Left to right: Liz Cook, Dr. Allen Breck as Father Kehler, Aaron Poley, Roxanne Morgan, Hannah Jorgenson, and Victoria Poley. *Cathedral archives.*

> years ago, the kitchen was directed by a part-time cook; last year two "cathedral caterers" served over 20,000 meals.[124]

In 1989 another national church paper wrote about how a maverick downtown cathedral flourishes in Denver:

> St. John's has been bucking the conventional wisdom which says inner-city churches without a neighborhood constituency must decline. . . . But under McPhail's leadership the parish has become a phenomenon, flourishing while other main-line churches are fading.[125]

As the 1980s progressed, things only got better. By 1989 the average attendance at Sunday services had almost reached the level attained in 1966. The

The clerical staff of St. John's Cathedral, ca. 1986. Left to right: Canon Rob O'Neill, Canon James Frensley, Canon David Morgan, Dean Donald McPhail, and Canon Ken Near. *Cathedral archives.*

Ordination of Sarah Butler as deacon on July 26, 1987. Left to right: Dean McPhail, Canon Morgan, Bishop Michael Marshall, Deacon Butler, and Deacon Jennifer Stiefel. *Courtesy, Colorado Episcopalian.*

Waiting for the 1986 bazaar to open. *Photo by Thomas M. Rowley. Cathedral archives.*

staff said that the facilities were not adequate for the programs of the parish, and a space study was undertaken. The resulting "Master-Planning" study recommended a $17 million expansion program. The cathedral was riding high, and the newspapers joined in the applause. The dean would soon discover that they were fair-weather friends, and the congregation had no inkling that a storm was gathering on the horizon.

During 1989 Dean McPhail was considered as a candidate for election as bishop in several dioceses. He was nominated for election in South Carolina and Arizona. He was not elected in the former but was elected as bishop coadjutor, on the first ballot in the diocese of Arizona. After consideration, he declined the call. He felt that for many personal reasons, and because of the way he per-

Donald Stewart McPhail,
seventh dean of St. John's
Cathedral, 1989. *Photo by Abdoo
Studios. Cathedral archives.*

ceived that the election was held, he should refuse, a decision that caused great
turmoil in Arizona and ultimately great turmoil in Dean McPhail's life. He was
a hands-on manager, who normally controlled his work environment; but the
problems in Arizona, combined with stress and exhaustion from overwork at St.
John's, created a disaster. Following several incidents of uncharacteristic behavior, and upon the advice and urging of Bishop Frey, Dean McPhail entered the
St. Barnabas Center for Clergy in Oconomowoc, Wisconsin, where he received
extensive psychological evaluation and treatment.

The congregation was devastated. Many members were outraged by his inappropriate public behavior. The vestry sponsored two Sunday afternoon meetings, called "The Hour of the Open Heart," so that parishioners could express their feelings about the situation. These seemed to have resulted in great division within the parish and lack of trust in each other. The harsh words spoken could not be taken back. The staff from St. Barnabas Center were scheduled to address the congregation about the situation, but the meeting was cancelled by the vestry. About the same time, an unofficial poll was sent to all of the congregation—about half of the hundreds of returned polls indicated the respondents wanted Dean McPhail to stay at the cathedral, but there was also a strong urging that he leave. In a sermon to the parish, Bishop Frey asked, "Are we the only army in the world to shoot our wounded?"[126]

In spite of considerable support, McPhail felt great pressure to resign. He soon submitted his resignation to the vestry to be effective after a one-year sabbatical. In the midst of all this, the Denver and Arizona media were unrelentingly harsh.

Donald McPhail faced an uncertain future upon leaving St. John's Cathedral, and his friend Bishop Ed Salmon, who could surely be described as a caring, concerned, courageous Christian, extended an invitation to the McPhails to come to the diocese of South Carolina. After a period serving as interim priest at Hilton Head and later at Charleston, Donald McPhail was elected rector of Grace Church in Charleston in 1992. This congregation is very caring and supportive, the parish is growing, the programs are exciting, McPhail is thriving, and his wife, Randy, is again enjoying the choir. In McPhail's own words, "I have experienced the good news that God can make a new mosaic out of the shattered stones of one's life."[127]

In early 1990 a search committee was formed to seek out a new dean. In July, canons Rob O'Neill and David Morgan were named co-priests-in-charge of St. John's. Four months later the Reverend Harvard Wilbur, retired rector from St. James Church, Wichita, Kansas (and for many years rector of the Chapel of Our Saviour in Colorado Springs), was named acting dean. The next ten months were a period of great difficulty at St. John's. The congregation was divided; some being glad that McPhail was gone, and others heartbroken that he had left. The vestry was both congratulated and cursed.

10. *The Kiblinger Years,*
1991–2000

ON JULY 29, 1991, THE VESTRY ELECTED the Reverend Charles E. Kiblinger II to be the next rector of St. John's and dean of the cathedral. The Kiblingers arrived in Denver on the first of October; and three weeks later he was instituted the twelfth rector of Saint John's Church in the Wilderness and installed the eighth dean of St. John's Cathedral. To affirm our being a part of a global community, the Very Reverend John F. Petty, provost of Coventry Cathedral, England, was asked to be preacher at this service.

Kiblinger was a native of Independence, Kansas. After ordination in Kansas City in 1966 and a first post in Shawnee, Kansas, Kiblinger served primarily in the South before coming to Denver. He was a teacher at Virginia Epis-

The Reverend
Charles Edward
Kiblinger,
dean-elect,
August, 1991.
Cathedral archives.

copal School and associate rector of St. Alban's Church in Annandale, Virginia (six years), and rector of St. James Church in Jackson, Mississippi (ten years), as well as being chaplain (eight years) at the University of the South in Sewanee, Tennessee.[128] He earned a master of divinity from Virginia Theological Seminary and a master of arts in clinical psychology from the Catholic University of America. He received an honorary doctor of divinity from the University of the South in 1996. Dean Kiblinger and his wife, Janet, a librarian, have two grown sons, William and Charles.

Kiblinger was concerned about reconciling the division he found at the cathedral following Donald McPhail's departure. As national president of the

The installation of Charles Kiblinger as rector of Saint John's Church in the
Wilderness and eighth dean of St. John's Cathedral, October 20, 1991. Left to
right: Canon David Morgan, Kiblinger, Bishop Jerry Winterrowd. *Cathedral archives.*

Community of the Cross of Nails and a companion of the Order of the CCN
at Coventry Cathedral, he was keenly familiar with the pastoral task of reconciliation. He initiated a reconciliation program, which was partially successful.
It addressed the needs of those who were angry with McPhail but failed to address the feelings of those who had supported him.

In February 1992, two new canons were hired. The Reverend Elizabeth
Boutwell Saulters from Jackson, Mississippi, was hired as canon educator. She
returned to Mississippi in August. The Reverend Joseph O. Robinson from Ya-
hoo City, Mississippi, was hired as canon presenter. He did his undergraduate

The dean's verger, Barry Bowman, leads the procession. *Cathedral archives.*

work in music, speech, and drama and completed his theological education at the University of the South located at Sewanee, Tennessee. Liturgy was his initial arena at the cathedral; however, he later was given the dual title of canon precentor/evangelist. Canon Robinson was elected dean of St. Andrew's Cathedral, Jackson, Mississippi, in September 1996. At that time Dean Kiblinger transferred the liturgical responsibility to Barry Bowman as full-time dean's verger.

February of 1992 also brought the Reverend Constance Delzell to the cathedral parish, when she was appointed interim vicar of St. Andrew's Church. In June she was named vicar of St. Andrew's and canon missioner of St. John's Cathedral. The Reverend Delzell, known as "Mother Connie," was the founding

Canon Missioner
Constance Delzell
in Dagwell Hall.
Cathedral communications.

vicar of St. Mary Magdalene in Boulder, from 1982 to 1989, and concurrently
served St. John's, Boulder, as assistant rector from 1982 to 1985. She is also the
founder and executive director of Children's Center for Arts & Learning
(CCAL), a program that fosters the academic and creative lives of children who
have been identified as being at risk at school. Born in Illinois, she transplanted
to Colorado and earned her undergraduate and graduate degrees at the University of Colorado, Boulder and at Iliff School of Theology. She and her husband, David, have a grown daughter, Heather, an artist who teaches at the
CCAL.[129] Mother Connie was the first woman to be ordained both deacon and
priest in the diocese of Colorado.

On October 30, 1999, fire struck St. Andrew's Church. It damaged the church's undercroft and fellowship hall and burned a hole in the floor of the main sanctuary. Worship services for the mission congregation were held at Temple Event Center, the former Temple Emanuel where St. John's held services in 1903 following the burning of the first cathedral. St. Andrew's was completely restored and its members celebrated the return to the church on May 24, 2000. At the diocesan convention in October 2000, St. Andrew's became a self-supporting parish.

On September 16, 1992, under Dean Kiblinger's direction, St. John's Cathedral parish began a new approach to adult Christian education—the Catechumenate, a way to explore the Christian faith in the Anglican tradition. This most successful program sets aside a period of eight or nine months for learning about Christianity, leading members to make a decision to be baptized or confirmed by the bishop on Easter Eve. The following year, the Catechesis of the Good Shepherd became part of the Christian education program for children age 3 to 12. Dean Kiblinger said, "The Catechesis of the Good Shepherd leads children into a more profound growth into Christ and his Church. It is by far the most creative and fulfilling children's program that I have seen in twenty-six years in the ministry."[130]

As the result of a retreat and subsequent task force study, the vestry decided to enlarge its membership in order to be more representative of the large congregation. From 1993 to 1995, seven posts on the vestry were added, bringing the vestry to fifteen members and two wardens.[131] At the same time Dean Kiblinger added to the mission of the vestry. While retaining its traditional functions along the lines of a corporate board, he placed an equal stress on the members' being spiritual leaders.

Elizabeth Penney Randall joined St. John's in 1988 and, after volunteering in the communications office for several months, joined the staff part time. During the summer of 1992 she assumed duties as director of Christian education. In June 1993, she was named lay canon educator for the Cathedral.

Air vent named "Folly" in Children's Garth. Painted by Mrs. Arnold (Dorothy) Vetter in 1995. *Cathedral archives.*

Being canon educator was a natural fit for Randall. A classics graduate of Smith College, she began teaching Latin and ancient history at Northfield Mount Hermon School in Northfield, Massachusetts. Later, she lived in Greece and taught English. While attending an Anglican church in Athens, she became a prison visitor, one of several activities to which she has contributed her time over the years. Other activities have included volunteering at a girls' home in Nicaragua, an animal shelter in Maine, and the St. Francis Center in Denver. Randall earned the master of divinity from Yale Divinity School.[132] She was ordained deacon in June 1994 and priest in December 1994. Canon Randall and her husband, Alan Gottlieb, are the parents of a daughter.

While pursuing careers in accounting and engineering library work, Colorado native Sarah Butler engaged in a lay ministry as president of the Daughters of the King and as a founding member of the Urban and Social Concerns Commission at St. John's. Canon Butler, deacon since 1987, was ordained priest in May 1994. She directed the Caring Ministers; lay parish minis-

Canon Educator
Elizabeth Randall.
*Cathedral
communications.*

ters; the Referral Service for seniors; and assisted Canon David Morgan with the Contemplative Prayer Outreach Fellowship.[133] She was named canon pastor, replacing Canon Morgan following his retirement in January 1996.

In October of that same year, when Canon Butler had just finished greeting worshipers after the 7:30 A.M. Sunday service, Barry Bowman, the dean's verger told her "the president is coming, and this is Mr. Eaves, his aide." Sarah looked a bit puzzled as she turned to the aide and asked, "The president of what?" "Of the United States," Mr. Eaves answered.[134] President Clinton had decided to worship at St. John's at the 9:00 A.M. Eucharist. Many in the congregation did not know the president was coming to St. John's until he walked down the aisle. Following the service, the president greeted parishioners as they left the service. All of them seemed thrilled that he had chosen to worship at St. John's. They appeared to be at ease with him and he with them, according to

Canon Pastor Sarah (Butler) Berlin conducts a service in the cathedral. *Cathedral communications.*

the verger. "He complimented the cathedral on the way we handled his visit and indicated to Canon Morgan that the morning had been a deeply spiritual experience for him."[135]

Canon Butler became Canon Sarah Berlin when she married the Reverend George Albert Berlin II on June 3, 2000.

The Reverend Stephen T. (Steve) Wilson was named canon evangelist of St. John's in January 1997, after serving as curate at St. Luke's Church in Montclair in east Denver and, before that, as youth minister at St. Bartholomew

President Clinton greets parishioners following the 9:00 A.M. Eucharist on
October 13, 1996. Canon-at-Large David Morgan on right. *Cathedral archives.*

Church, Atlanta. A fourth-generation Episcopalian and native Denverite, he and
his family made the requisite moves in his youth as his father, also an Episcopal
priest, served a number of churches along the Front Range. While earning a degree at the London School of Economics, he volunteered at Center Point, an
emergency youth shelter in Soho. In Denver he has volunteered at the St. Francis
Center for eleven years.[136] The Reverend Wilson received his master of divinity
degree from Seabury-Western School of Theology in Evanston, Illinois. He was
ordained deacon at St. John's in mid-1995; and in December of that year he was
ordained to the priesthood at St. Luke's Church. In 1998, Canon Wilson married

Canon Evangelist
Stephen T. Wilson.
*Cathedral
communications.*

parishioner Maria Rhine in the cathedral. Their first child was born in August
of 2000.

Canon Wilson is responsible for many innovative programs at St. John's:
a new thrust for the Evangelism Commission, which has organized parishioners
in several neighborhoods for fellowship and improved communication; the 20s
and 30s Ministry, with its own Sunday evening service; the Habitat for Humanity and the Holy Hammers project, which involves parishioners from St. John's
and other churches to build homes for qualified families; and extending the
same principle overseas, volunteers from St. John's have journeyed to the Do-
minican Republic, Guatemala, and Cuba to build schools and housing.[137]

Among the many wonderful assets that Dean Kiblinger found when he arrived at St. John's was Don Pearson, organist and choirmaster. At this writing, as Pearson begins his twentieth year at the cathedral, a look at his accomplishments is in order.[138] There have been many awards and honors bestowed on Pearson and the music department—among them we find: Best Classical Recital and Best Classical Performance from Westword magazine, Distinguished Alumni award from the University of Wisconsin, Colorado Conductor of the Year (1992) from the Colorado American Choral Director Association, guest organist and guest conductor with the Denver Chamber Orchestra, and an invitation to the choir to sing at St. Thomas Church in New York City.[139] Since 1981, St. John's concert series has hosted tens of thousands of guests each year with scores of choirs, organists, and choir and orchestra concerts. St. John's choir has produced eight recording projects with a major recording company. From the Denver *Rocky Mountain News,* "The 75 voice choir is the third-most-recorded [church] choir in America, behind only St. Thomas in New York and the Mormon Tabernacle Choir."[140]

In August of 1998, at the national conference held in Denver, the Organ Historical Society presented the cathedral with a certificate stating that the Kimball Organ "has been selected for recognition as an instrument of exceptional historic merit worthy of preservation."[141]

In 1998, after more than two years' work by the Master Plan Committee, copies of their report were made available to the congregation. In describing this report, the director of development, John Hoskins wrote, "The Master Plan for St. John's Cathedral is a wonderful road map that addresses the building needs well into the next century."[142]

Following approval by the vestry, March 21, 1999 became the kickoff date for the Capital Fund Campaign for the first phase of the Master Plan. This phase included: rebuilding the front steps of the cathedral adding ramps for handicapped accessibility; a new connector building, called the Memorial Hall,

Don Pearson
conducting
the music at
an Easter service
at St. John's.
Cathedral archives.

St. John's choir
member Jean
Martin, former
secretary to Dean
Roberts. *Cathedral
archives.*

The "On this Rock" capital fund campaign for the first phase of the Master Plan featured the cornerstone of the 1881 cathedral. *Woodward collection.*

between the cathedral and the Roberts building to relieve the bottleneck at the southeast door of the church; a new and clearly identifiable entrance from the west parking lot; new facilities for the music department in the basement of the Roberts building; new classrooms on the first floor; an elevator serving all floors of the building; and large and accessible rest rooms. (The new use of the basement of the Roberts Building marked the end of the St. John's Bazaar.) Other projects, funded separately, include the expansion of All Souls' Walk and the refurbishing of St. Martin's Chapel. The congregation responded enthusiastically by pledging funds in excess of four million dollars. The front steps and ramps were dedicated in March of 2000. The other projects are in progress at this writing. The Master Plan is designed to be implemented over a period of fifteen years, so many more changes lie ahead for the cathedral.

In 2000, St. John's Cathedral celebrated 140 years of ministering to the city of Denver. A number of special events commemorated the anniversary, be-

Demolition of old clergy sacristy at site of new connector building. Columbarium in the fore-ground. *Woodward collection.*

ginning with the annual meeting on January 29, 2000, exactly 140 years after the first service held in Denver by Father Kehler. March saw the new Denver Bach-Fest, a series of six concerts dedicated to the music of J. S. Bach. The Reverend Herbert M. Barrall, former dean of the cathedral, was invited back in May to preach at the Kirkin 'o' the Tartan, the festive service he introduced to the cathedral in the 1960s. In June, members of Temple Emanuel, with which St. John's has shared a long and cordial relationship, attended evensong, followed by an ice cream social. In July, St. John's served as host church for the Triennial General Convention of the Episcopal Church and sponsored a number of special events at the convention center and the cathedral. This was the third national convention to be held in Denver (the others being in 1931 and 1979).

St. John's Day, in September, saw another special evensong, this time in observance of social justice. The opening Eucharist for the diocesan convention and the annual Blessing of the Animals were held in October. All Saints' Sunday, November 5, 2000, with worship services and a special concert marked

Former
Dean
Herbert M.
Barrall at
new front
steps of
cathedral,
May 2000.
*Woodward
collection.*

exactly the anniversary of the first service held in the present cathedral seventy-nine years ago. In December the 140th anniversary celebration was concluded with a festive holiday gala at the Denver Design Center.

In the midst of this anniversary year, Dean Charles Kiblinger resigned as dean and rector of the parish to accept the position of director of leadership and ministry development at Virginia Theological Seminary, his alma mater. His last Sunday at the cathedral was on August 15, 2000. Following his leaving, the Reverend E. M. "Bert" Womack Jr., canon to the ordinary of the diocese of Colorado was named interim dean.

And so at the conclusion of the cathedral's 141st year, the beginning of the liturgical year, the end of a century, and the outset of a new millennium, St. John's has once more formed a search committee to embark on selecting a new rector and dean to perpetuate the traditions of the church and to promote the forward-looking mission of Saint John's Church in the Wilderness.

Interim Dean
E. M. "Bert"
Womack Jr.
Cathedral
communications.

Glossary

Definitions of terms used in this book are taken generally from *A Dictionary of the Episcopal Church*, comp., Rolfe P. Crum, 8th ed., Baltimore, Trefoil Publishing Society, 1951. A few definitions are from *Webster's New World Dictionary of the American Language*, 2nd ed., New York, Simon & Schuster, 1984. Additions to the definitions for this book about St. John's Cathedral are by the author. Within definitions, other terms defined in this listing are italicized.

Aisle   The passageway on either side of the *nave*, separated from it by columns and arches.

Altar   The table upon which the eucharistic Elements (bread and wine) are consecrated. The chief altar is elevated above the rest of the church (hence called the "high altar"). The freestanding altar is positioned in the *chancel* so that the priest may stand behind it facing the congregation.

Altar Rail   The railing that encloses the *sanctuary* surrounding the *altar* at which communicants kneel to receive the bread and wine of *Holy Communion*.

Anglican Communion   Those Churches which are in communion with the Church of England and hold the same faith, order, and worship. The *Episcopal Church of America* is part of the Anglican Communion.

Anglo-Catholic   A member of the Anglican Church who stresses its continuous tradition with the Roman Catholic Church before and after the Reformation. In this book it is used to mean *high church*. See *Catholic*.

Apse   The semicircular end of the chancel containing the *sanctuary* and *altar*.

Baptism, Holy   The rite by which a person is admitted into the fellowship of Christ's religion, that is, the Church.

Baptistry   The space set aside for the baptismal font. Sometimes a separate building.

Belfry   The place where the church bells are hung.

Bishop   The highest of the three orders of the sacred ministry (bishops, priests and deacons). The bishops are the successors of the Apostles and give validity to the ministry of the Church. See *diocesan, missionary bishop, coadjutor bishop, suffragan bishop,* and *presiding bishop.*

Bishop and Chapter   The organization created to manage the *missionary district* and later the *diocese;* no longer in existence.

Board of Missions, Domestic Committee of   The national organization that supported the *missionary bishops;* no longer in existence.

Campanile   A bell tower built separately from the church.

Canon   (1) A law of the Church set forth by an ecclesiastical council or *convention;* (2) A member of the *clergy* who is connected with a cathedral as a member of the staff to assist the *dean;* (3) A member of the clergy who is connected with a cathedral as a member of the *chapter* appointed by the *bishop;* (4) A member of the clergy who is a member of the diocesan staff to assist the bishop.

Canonical   According to the canons or laws of the church.

Canonical Residence   The ecclesiastical connection of a member of the *clergy* with a certain *diocese* or *bishop.*

Canopy   The rooflike projection over the rear choir stall.

Cathedra   The bishop's chair or throne.

Cathedral   The principal church of the *diocese* where the *bishop* has his *cathedra.*

Cathedral Chapter   See *bishop and chapter.*

Catholic   Literally meaning "universal" or "embracing all." The Episcopal Church is part of the Catholic Church, which is not to be confused with the Roman Catholic Church.

Celebrant   The bishop or priest who celebrates the *Holy Communion.*

Chancel   That part of the church containing the *sanctuary* and the *choir* and seats for the *Clergy* and choristers.

Chapel A sanctuary adjacent to a church or cathedral; or a separate house of worship dependent upon a parish church, a cathedral, or a diocese.

Chaplain A member of the *clergy* who has full-time or part-time duty in ministering to the religious needs of a school, a hospital, or a military establishment.

Chapter A meeting of the *canons* of a cathedral. See *bishop and chapter.*

Chapter House The "house" (building) in which the *canons* meet.

Choir That portion of the *chancel* of a cathedral or church where the choristers sit.

Church "The Church is the Body of which Jesus Christ is the Head and all baptized people are the members." Also a church building or house of worship.

Clerestory The upper part of the *nave* of a church or cathedral, which rises above the aisles and has an arcade of windows.

Clergy A collective name for those ordained to the threefold ministry of the Church (*bishops, priests,* and *deacons*).

Cloister A covered walk on the grounds of a church or cathedral.

Close Enclosed grounds around or beside a cathedral.

Coadjutor, Bishop A bishop who is elected to assist the bishop of a *diocese* and who, upon the latter's death or resignation, succeeds him in office.

Columbarium A depository, sometimes a walkway (as at St. John's) or wall, with niches for urns containing the ashes of cremated bodies.

Communion, Holy The sacrament of the Lord's Supper, which was ordained by Christ for a continual remembrance of the sacrifice of the death of Christ and of the benefits we receive thereby.

Communicant A baptized and confirmed member of the Church in good standing.

Confirmation An ordinance of the Church, sacramental in character and grace conferring. It is the completion of *baptism.*

Consecration   (1) The dedication of anything to divine service; the setting apart of a church or other place by a bishop to be used for the service of God; (2) The advancement of a presbyter who has been duly elected and qualified to the rank of *bishop*; (3) The act of blessing and invoking the Divine Presence upon the Elements of the *Holy Communion*.

Convention   A meeting of clerical and lay delegates. A diocesan convention meets annually, whereas the General Convention of the National Church meets once in three years.

Crossing   At St. John's, this generally refers to the cross-aisle at the halfway point of the nave. See *Transept*.

Crucifer   One who carries the processional cross in front of an ecclesiastical procession.

Crypt   An underground portion of a church used as a *Chapel*; and sometimes for burials.

Curate   One who assists the *Rector* in the parish. In this book, the term "assistant to the rector" is used.

Deacon   The first and lowest order of the three orders of the ministry (diaconate). A deacon may assist a priest at the *Holy Communion* in the administration to the communicants but may not consecrate the Elements.

Deaconess   A member of the order of women trained and set apart by a religious service for the work of the Church (prior to 1970).

Dean   (1) The presiding dignitary of a *cathedral*; (2) The president of a district of a *diocese*; (3) The head of the faculty of a college or theological seminary.

Deanery   The residence provided for the *dean* of a cathedral.

Dimissory Letter   A letter of transfer.

Diocesan   Pertaining to a *diocese*; a bishop who is in charge of a diocese.

Diocese   The limits of jurisdiction of a diocesan bishop.

Eagle   The emblem of St. John the Evangelist.

East, The   The altar is ecclesiastically at the eastern end of the church (the historical direction regardless of actual compass direction).

Ecclesiastical   Of the Church.

Emeritus   An honorary title indicating retired from service, but retaining one's rank.

Episcopacy   That type of church government in which bishops are the chief pastors, with priests and deacons under them.

Episcopal Church, The   The usual name of that branch of the *Anglican Communion* in the United States, although the full name is the "Protestant Episcopal Church in the United States of America." It is called Episcopal because it possesses the Historic Episcopate (i.e., bishops in the order of the Apostolical Succession).

Epistle Side   That side of the altar from which the Epistle is read; the left side of the priest as he faces the congregation, known ecclesiastically as the south side.

Eucharist, Holy   The service of *Holy Communion* or Lord's Supper.

Eucharistic Vestments   The special vestments worn in celebrating the *Holy Eucharist*.

Evangelical   Belonging to, or consistent with the Gospels. In this book, it is used to denote *low church*.

Father   A title sometimes given to a parish *priest*. (Some women ordained to the priesthood have adopted "Mother," but many women priests as well as parishioners find this awkward).

Flying Buttress   A buttress connected with a wall at some distance from it by an arch that serves to resist outward pressure.

Frontal   A piece of material hung in front of the *altar* and reaching to the floor. Also the front screen of choir stalls or pews.

Gallery   A platform or projecting upper floor attached to the back wall or sides of a church.

Garth   An enclosed yard or garden.

Gospel Side   The side of the altar from which the Gospel is read; the right side of the priest as he faces the congregation, known ecclesiastically as the north side.

Gothic A style of architecture developed in western Europe between the twelfth and sixteenth centuries, characterized by the use of ribbed vaulting, flying buttresses, pointed arches, and steep high roofs.

High Church A part of the Anglican Church that emphasizes the importance of the (male) priesthood and of traditional rituals and doctrines. Also associated with an elaborate style of liturgical worship emphasizing music and ritual actions.

Laity The people of the congregation as distinguished from the *clergy.*

Lectern The stand upon which the Bible is placed, from which are read the Scripture lessons for the day.

Liturgy The rituals governing the conduct of worship services of the Church.

Low Church A part of the Anglican Church that attaches less importance to the priesthood and to traditional rituals, and more importance to the Gospels. Associated with a less elaborate style of worship.

Mission A group of church members which is not self-supporting but is dependent upon a *parish* or *diocese.*

Missionary Bishop A *bishop* elected by General Convention of the House of Bishops and consecrated to exercise Episcopal functions in areas not organized into dioceses.

Missionary District The limits of jurisdiction of a *missionary bishop.*

Narthex A vestibule stretching across the western end of a cathedral, separated from the *nave* by a wall and under the gallery. At St. John's, the narthex is at the north end of the building fronting 14th Avenue.

Nave The body of the church building in front of the *chancel* and between the aisles, where the congregation sits. It is called "nave" because the Church is oftentimes depicted in sacred art as a ship moving heavenward. *See vaulting.*

Ordination The act of setting apart to the sacred ministry by the laying on of hands by the bishop. *Deacons* and *priests* are ordained (whereas bishops are consecrated).

Parish A unit of a *diocese,* usually with a church building or buildings, having a name of its own and a charter from the state.

Parish House   A building other than the church proper where the educational and social work of a parish can be carried on.

Parishioner   A member of a *parish, chapel,* or *mission.*

Pastor   A minister placed in charge of the spiritual care of a *parish* or *congregation.*

Pew   A low bench with a fixed back and kneelers for use by worshippers.

Presbyter   One who, having served his or her diaconate, has been ordained to the second order of the sacred ministry, i.e., the priesthood.

Presiding Bishop   The president of the National Council of the Episcopal Church, who presides over the House of Bishops and the General Convention.

Prie-Dieu   A small desk arranged to support a book and with a footpiece on which to kneel, similar to a prayer desk.

Priesthood   The second order of the sacred ministry. The word "priest" is a shortened form of the word "presbyter" and is used to emphasize the sacerdotal character of the order. A priest may offer the Holy Sacrifice in the Eucharist and officiate at any of the other sacraments and services of the Prayer Book except Holy *Confirmation, Ordination,* and *Consecration,* which are the functions of a bishop.

Pro-Cathedral   Where there is no cathedral, a parish church is sometimes selected for this purpose by the bishop.

Protestant   A term loosely applied to all Christian denominations (and their members) that are not Roman Catholic or Orthodox.

Protestant Episcopal Church in the United States of America, The   The full name of that portion of the *Anglican Communion* in the United States.

Pulpit   The structure in a church consisting of a platform with a railing and a reading desk, from which the sermon is delivered.

Rector   A member of the *clergy* who is in charge of a *parish.*

Rector's Assistant (Assistant to the Rector)   An ordained person appointed by the *rector* to help in the work of the parish.

Rectory   The residence provided for the *Rector*.

Reredos   A back screen, usually of carved wood or stone, which surmounts the *altar*.

Reverend, The   The title given to an ordained member of the *clergy*. It is an adjective, and should be preceded by "the" and, as a form of address, should be followed by a Mr., Mrs., Ms., Dr., or Canon, and so on, or by the name in full.

Reverend, The Right   Customary title given to a *bishop*.

Reverend, The Very   Customary title given to a *dean*.

Rood   A cross or crucifix.

Rood Screen   The screen supporting a cross, separating the *chancel* from the *nave*.

Romanesque   A style of architecture characterized chiefly by rounded arches and massive stonework. Based on a style of European architecture of the eleventh and twelfth centuries.

Sacerdotal   Belief in the divine authority of the priesthood.

Sacrament   An ordinance that possesses "an outward and visible sign of an inward and spiritual grace," e.g., *baptism* and *Holy Communion*.

Sacristy   The room in the church building in which the vestments, books, and sacred vessels are kept, and preparation is made for services.

Sanctuary   A portion of the *chancel* behind the altar rail.

Seminary, Theological   A school of preparation for candidates for *ordination*.

Sexton   A lay officer of the parish among whose duties are to open and shut the church buildings and to keep them clean, under the direction of the *rector*.

Stall   A seat on either side of the *chancel* with a back and armrests for the use of the *clergy*; a long bench with back and ends placed lengthwise of the choir portion of the *chancel* for seating the choristers, called choir stalls.

Standing Committee   A permanent committee in every *diocese* or *missionary district*, elected by the diocesan convention, whose duties are to act as the bishop's advising council and to pass upon legal matters, and other specific duties prescribed by the general and the diocesan canons.

Suffragan Bishop　A *bishop* elected to assist the bishop of the diocese but without the right of succession to his office.

Tracery　Ornamental work, as in a *Gothic* window or vaulting.

Transept　The two wings of a cruciform (cross-shaped) church representing the arms of the cross and intersecting the *nave* at the foot of the *chancel,* at what is called the crossing in church architecture.

Undercroft　A subterranean room or chapel under a church; a *crypt.* The present St. John's Cathedral has no undercroft.

Vaulting　Arched construction of masonry, forming a ceiling.

Verger　One who carries the verge or staff in procession before a dignitary.

Vestments　The garments worn by the *clergy* and all who assist in Divine Service.

Vestry　(1) The room within the church building where clergy put on vestments; (2) The organization for the management of financial and secular affairs of the parish. It is made up of those elected or appointed to represent the parish together with the *rector* and the *wardens.*

Vicar　One who has charge of a *chapel* or *mission* as representing the *rector* of the parish or the *bishop* of the diocese.

Wainscot　Paneling on the walls of the *chancel* behind the choir stalls.

Wardens　Two lay officers of a *parish* distinguished by the titles "Senior Warden" and "Junior Warden." At this time, both wardens at St. John's are elected by the parish.

The Clergy of Saint John's Church in the Wilderness

Bold type indicates rectors and deans. Parentheses indicate function served, not position title.

NAME	POSITION	FROM	TO
John Henrich Kehler	**Founder and first rector**	Jan 1860	Jun 1862
	Acting rector	Oct 1864	1864
	(assisting minister)	1865	1875
Isaac A. Hagar, deacon	Acting rector	Jul 1862	Dec 1862
Horace Baldwin Hitchings	(Rector elect)	Nov 1862	Aug 1863
	Rector	Aug 1863	Jan 1869
	Rector emeritus	Mar 1910	Apr 1917
George Maxwell Randall, bishop	**Rector**	Apr 1869	Sept 1873
Samuel Johnson French	Assistant to the rector	Aug 1869	May 1871
Henry Hobart DeGarmo	Assistant to the rector	Jul 1871	Aug 1871
Walter Howard Moore	Assistant to the rector	Jul 1871	May 1872
	Acting rector	Oct 1873	Mar 1874
	Asst. in charge of Trinity Memorial Chapel	Mar 1874	Jan 1875
C. E. Butler	(assisting minister)	Mar 1872	Jul 1872
P. Voorhees Finch	**Rector**	Mar 1874	Mar 1879

NAME	POSITION	FROM	TO
Henry Martyn Hart	**Rector**	Sept 1879	Oct 1879
	Rector and first dean	Oct 1879	Mar 1920
J. B. Alexander	Assistant to the rector	Dec 1880	Apr 1881
Charles Edward Dandridge	Assistant to the rector	Feb 1884	Sept 1884
David Douglas Wallace	Assistant to the rector	Mar 1885	Jun 1886
J. Eldred Brown	(assisting minister)	1887	1887
William Charles Bradshaw	(assisting minister)	1888	1889
James C. Kemm	Assistant to the rector	Nov 1889	Jul 1890
Dan Lewis	Minor canon	Oct 1890	Oct 1893
Pelham Williams	(assisting minister)	Jun 1891	1891
Francis Byrne	Canon	Jan 1892	1900
	Honorary canon (retired and assisting)	1900	Jun 1904
Frank Evans Badger	Assistant to the rector	Jan 1894	1894
Charles Winfred Douglas	Minor canon	Sept 1894	1896
	(returned)	1934	1944
Charles J. H. Mockridge	Minor canon	1897	1899
Ernest Frederick Smith	Minor canon to St. Andrew's Mission	Oct 1897	1898
Arnold George Henry Bode	Minor canon to St. Andrew's Mission	1900	May 1901
Edward Lyman Eustis	Minor canon to St. Andrew's Mission	Sept 1901	Apr 1904
Miss Jessica Martin	Deaconess	1903	1903
A. A. Pruden, Army Chaplain, Wyoming	(assisting minister)	Sept 1904	Aug 1905
Miss Metzler	Deaconess	1905	1905
George H. Holoran	Assistant to the rector	Feb 1906	Jan 1907
Caleb Irving Mills	Assistant to the rector	Aug 1907	1908

NAME	POSITION	FROM	TO
Dana C. Colegrove	Assistant to the rector	1911	Mar 1913
George Gallup	Minor canon	May 1913	Jan 1914
John William Jones	Minor canon	Sept 1914	Feb 1916
Claude Williard Sprouse	(lay assistant)	Sept 1916	Apr 1917
	Assistant to the rector	May 1917	Dec 1917
Elvon L. Tull	Assistant to the rector	Jun 1918	Jun 1919
Sherman Coolidge	Canon	Feb 1919	1926
	Honorary canon	1926	Jan 1932
Frederick F. Beckerman	Canon	Jun 1919	Jan 1922
	Acting rector	Mar 1920	Jul 1921
	(assisting minister)	Jun 1922	Oct 1922
Albert P. Mack	(assisting minister)	Jan 1921	1921
Duncan Hodge Browne	**Rector and dean**	Jul 1921	Mar 1924
Ralph V. Hinkle	Assistant to the rector	Feb 1923	Oct 1923
Ernest Wetherill Wood	Acting rector	Mar 1924	May 1924
Army Chaplain,	(assisting minister)	Dec 1926	Feb 1927
Fort Logan			
Benjamin Dunlap Dagwell	**Rector and dean**	Jun 1924	Jan 1936
	(returned)	1962	
Jonathan Watson	Canon	Sept 1924	Dec 1926
	Honorary Canon	Jan 1927	Apr 1927
Harry Watts	Canon to St. Michaels &		
	All Angels Mission	Aug 1925	Sept 1928
	Canon	Sept 1928	Mar 1959
	Bishop's vicar	Apr 1957	Sept 1957
	Canon emeritus	Apr 1959	Dec 1986
Wallace Bristor	Canon	Apr 1927	Sept 1928

NAME	POSITION	FROM	TO
Jerome L. Fritsche	Asst. to St. Michaels & All Angels Mission	Sept 1928	Nov 1930
William Leonard Blaker	(assisting minister)	Nov 1930	1930
Edwin James Skinner	(assisting minister)	1932	1932
Charles Winfred Douglas	Honorary canon	Jan 1934	Jan 1944
Frederick Warren Oakes	Honorary canon	1934	1944
Paul Roberts	**Rector and dean**	Jan 1936	Apr 1957
	Dean emeritus	Jan 1959	Mar 1984
Vine Victor Deloria Sr.	Domestic missionary, South Dakota	Nov 1938	Oct 1951
Richard C. Rogers	Assistant to the rector	Jun 1940	Sept 1941
John Samuel Foster	Honorary canon	1944	1944
Gerrit Smith Barnes	Deacon	Dec 1946	May 1952
	Assistant to St. John's Mission	May 1952	Oct 1952
	Canon	Oct 1952	Nov 1955
Ainsley Maxwell Carlton	Deacon	Sept 1947	Oct 1947
	Canon to St. Paul's Mission	Oct 1947	Jan 1949
	Honorary canon	Jan 1949	Apr 1950
Paul James Habliston	(lay assistant-youth director)	Feb 1949	Sept 1949
	Deacon (youth director)	Sept 1949	Mar 1950
	Canon (youth director)	Mar 1950	Nov 1951
Harold S. Jones	Domestic missionary, South Dakota	Nov 1951	May 1956
Vernon Myers	Assistant to rector (youth director)	Mar 1952	Oct 1952
	Canon	Oct 1952	Sept 1957
	Canon to Saint Philip & Saint James Mission	Sept 1957	Jun 1958
Harold A. Magee	Canon	Jan 1956	Sept 1957

NAME	POSITION	FROM	TO
Cecil L. Franklin	Assistant to the rector	Apr 1957	May 1958
Eric Alfred Clifford Smith	(assisting minister)	Aug 1957	1957
Frank R. Myers	(assisting minister)	Sept 1957	1957
William Sentelle Lea	**Rector**	Sept 1957	Oct 1957
	Rector and dean	Oct 1957	Dec 1962
Bruce Walker Ravenel	Canon	Mar 1958	Dec 1960
	(returned)	1977	1984
Russell Kaoru Nakata	Canon	Apr 1958	Jan 1983
	Priest in charge	Jul 1980	Mar 1981
	Honorary clergy associate	Jan 1983	Jan 1989
	Canon emeritus	Feb 1989	Sept 1996
Herbert Monroe Barrall Jr.	Canon	Jun 1959	Feb 1963
	(became rector)	1963	1980
Philip Morton Gresham	Canon	Feb 1961	May 1964
Benjamin D. Dagwell retired bishop	Acting dean	Feb 1962	Apr 1962
Herbert Monroe Barrall Jr.	**Rector**	Feb 1963	Sept 1963
	Rector and dean	Sept 1963	Jun 1980
C. Arch Hopper	Parish visitor	Aug 1963	Apr 1967
	Volunteer associate	May 1967	Jul 1968
	Volunteer associate	Dec 1969	1971
Frank Rowley	Canon	Jun 1964	Jan 1979
	Honorary canon	Jun 1981	Sept 1982
Llewellyn Wallace Wells Jr.	Canon	Jul 1965	Jul 1977
Richard Lawrence Sonne	Volunteer associate	May 1967	1977
Eric Alfred Clifford Smith	Volunteer associate	May 1967	May 1969
Richard Taylor Lyford	Parish visitor	Jul 1968	Jan 1974
Remey Leland Clem	Volunteer associate	Feb 1969	1977

NAME	POSITION	FROM	TO
Bruce Walker Ravenel	Canon	Aug 1977	Apr 1984
Gerald Schnackenberg	Deacon in training	Aug 1977	Dec 1977
John Wengrovius	Deacon in training	Aug 1977	Dec 1977
Kate Spelman Knapp	Assisting deacon	Jun 1979	Dec 1979
Peter George Castano	Parish visitor	Jul 1979	1980
Donald Stewart McPhail	**Rector and dean**	Mar 1981	Mar 1991
Robert John O'Neill	Canon	Jul 1981	Aug 1991
	Co-priest-in-charge	Jul 1990	Nov 1990
David Forbes Morgan	Assisting deacon	Mar 1982	Oct 1982
	Canon	Nov 1982	Jan 1992
	Co-priest-in-charge	Jul 1990	Nov 1990
	Canon pastor	Feb 1992	Dec 1995
	Canon-at-large	Jan 1996	Present
Paul George Robinson	Deacon intern	Jun 1983	Dec 1983
	Canon	Jan 1984	Apr 1984
James Monroe Frensley	Canon	Nov 1984	Mar 1987
Kenneth Mark Near	Canon	Jan 1985	Nov 1986
	Canon and vicar of St. Andrew's Church	Dec 1986	Oct 1991
Sarah Aline Butler	Assisting deacon	Jul 1987	Jul 1990
	Canon	Aug 1990	Dec 1995
	Canon pastor	Jan 1996	Jun 2000
Sarah Aline Berlin	Canon pastor	Jun 2000	Present
Richard Neal Shackleford	Canon	Jul 1988	Sept 1991
Wallace Bruce Clift Jr.	Honorary clergy associate	Oct 1988	Present
Jean Dalby Clift	Honorary clergy associate	Oct 1988	Present
Elton William Pounds	Honorary clergy associate	Oct 1989	Jun 1997
Henry Jesse	Honorary clergy associate	Jun 1990	Feb 1999
	Assisting priest	Mar 1999	Present

NAME	POSITION	FROM	TO
Ernest Harry Priest	Honorary clergy associate	Jun 1990	Dec 1990
	Interim vicar of		
	St. Andrew's Church	Nov 1991	Feb 1992
	Assisting priest	Sept 1993	Dec 1995
	Honorary clergy associate	Jan 1996	Present
Norman Hugh Barbour	Honorary clergy associate	Aug 1990	Present
Harvard L. Wilbur Jr.	Acting dean	Nov 1990	Sept 1991
	Honorary clergy associate	Aug 1992	Oct 1993
Charles Edward Kiblinger II	**Rector and dean**	Oct 1991	Aug 2000
Joseph Oliver Robinson	Canon precentor	Feb 1992	Dec 1995
	Canon precentor/evangelist	Jan 1996	Sept 1996
Elizabeth Boutwell Saulters	Canon educator	Feb 1992	Aug 1992
James R. Anderson	Honorary clergy associate	Feb 1992	Jun 1992
Constance Kay Delzell	Interim vicar of		
	St. Andrew's Church	Feb 1992	Jun 1992
	Canon missioner and vicar		
	of St. Andrew's Church	Jul 1992	Oct 2000
James C. Lewis	Honorary clergy associate	Dec 1992	Apr 1995
Marie Elizabeth Shirer	Honorary clergy associate	May 1993	Jul 1997
Mary Joan Delaney	Honorary clergy associate	Oct 1993	Present
Elizabeth Penny Randall	Canon educator	Aug 1994	Present
Marilyn Butler Schneider	Deacon, St. Andrew's Church	Aug 1994	Dec 1994
Stephen Thomas Wilson	Canon evangelist	Jan 1997	Present
Sally Simms Brown	Deacon, St. Andrew's Church	Aug 1997	Oct 2000
Carmen Marlene Stansberry	Honorary clergy associate	Dec 1997	Sept 1998
Rebecca Ferrell Nickel	Curate, St. Andrew's Church	Jun 1998	Apr 1999
Thomas H. Troeger	Honorary clergy associate	Nov 1999	Present
E. M. "Bert" Womack Jr.	Interim dean	Sept 2000	Present

The Canons of the Bishop and Chapter of the Cathedral of Saint John the Evangelist

The Bishop and Chapter of the Cathedral of Saint John the Evangelist was the corporation that functioned as the board of trustees of church property consisting of Matthews Hall, Jarvis Hall, Wolfe Hall, and the Board of Missions. The canons were appointed by Bishop Spalding and Bishop Olmsted from the creation of the chapter in 1880 until the diocese reorganized in 1915.

The residential canons had charge of education, parochial, missionary, or charitable work in the city of Denver or vicinity. The honorary canons were generally rural deans. Although the bishops intended for these canons to have "seats" at the cathedral, they were not assistants to Dean Hart, nor were they employees of the cathedral.

NAME	APPOINTED	TERM	POSITION
H. H. Haynes	Residential canon	1880–1881	Principal, Jarvis Hall
G. T. LeBoutillier	Honorary canon	1880–1883	Rector, Grace, Colorado Springs
C. H. Marshall	Honorary canon	1880	Rector, Trinity Memorial, Denver
	Residential canon	1881–1895	Rector, Trinity Memorial, Denver
		1896–1915	Rector, St. Barnabas, Denver
M. F. Sorenson	Honorary canon	1880	Rector, St. Paul's, Littleton
	Residential canon	1881–1882	Rector, St. Paul's, Littleton
	Honorary canon	1883–1885	Rector, St. Paul's, Littleton
	Residential canon	1886–1887	Rector, All Saints', Denver

NAME	APPOINTED	TERM	POSITION
O. E. Ostenson	Residential canon	1881–1882	Rector, Emmanuel, Denver
	Honorary canon	1883–1885	Rector, St. Stephen's, Longmont
		1886–1889	Rector, St. John's, Ouray
		1890–1892	Rector, St. Matthew's, Grand Junction
G. C. Rafter	Honorary canon	1881–1883	Rector, Calvary, Golden
John Gray	Residential canon	1882	Rector, All Saints', Denver
E. H. Gaynor	Honorary canon	1884	Rector, St. Peter's, Pueblo
G. Forrester	Residential canon	1885–1886	Canon missioner
	Honorary canon	1887–1888	Rector, St. Andrew's, La Junta
A. B. Hunter	Residential canon	1886	Rector, Emmanuel, Denver
		1887	Chaplain, Wolfe Hall
A. R. Kieffer	Honorary canon	1886–1893	Rector, Grace, Colorado Springs
D. D. Wallace	Residential canon	1887–1891	Rector, Emmanuel, Denver
		1892–1894	Chaplain/Supt., St. Luke's Hospital
A. W. Arundel	Residential canon	1887–1891	Rector, St. Mark's, Denver
S. M. Holden	Residential canon	1888	Principal, Jarvis Hall
A. G. Singsen	Residential canon	1888	Rector, All Saints', Denver
J. A. Antrim	Honorary canon	1888	Rector, St. George's, Leadville
Alexander Allen	Honorary canon	1889	Rector, Christ, Aspen
John C. S. Weills	Honorary canon	1890–1892	Rector, St. Andrew's, Manitou
A. L. Williams	Residential canon	1891	Rector, St. Paul's, Denver
Edward J. Harper	Honorary canon	1891	Rector, St. George's, Leadville
Amos Bannister	Honorary canon	1891	Rector, St. Thomas', Alamosa
John Wallace Ohl	Honorary canon	1891–1905	Rector, Ascension, Salida
		1906–1908	Rector, Holy Trinity, Pueblo
	Residential canon	1912–1914	Rector, St. Thomas', Denver
J. H. Houghton	Residential canon	1893–1915	Rector, St. Mark's, Denver
E. P. Newton	Honorary canon	1893–1902	Rector, Holy Trinity, Pueblo

NAME	APPOINTED	TERM	POSITION
J. W. Colwell	Honorary canon	1894–1895	Rector, Grace, Colorado Springs
F. W. Oakes	Residential canon	1895–1896	Rector, All Saints', Denver
		1897–1915	Superintendent, The Home
R. S. Radcliffe	Honorary canon	1895	Rector, Ascension, Salida
		1896–1897	General missionary
		1898–1899	Archdeacon
Fred F. Kramer	Honorary canon	1895–1896	Rector, St. John's, Boulder
	Residential canon	1897–1911	Rector, All Saints', Denver
Charles Ysla Grimes	Residential canon	1897–1900	Rector, Trinity Memorial, Denver
		1901	Archdeacon
A. B. Jennings	Residential canon	1897–1901	Rector, St. Stephen's, Denver
P. H. Hickman	Honorary canon	1897	Rector, St. John's, Boulder
		1898	Rector, St. Mark's, Evergreen
Frank W. Henry	Honorary canon	1899	Rector, Trinity, Greeley
E. W. Sibbald	Honorary canon	1900–1909	Rector, St. John's, Boulder
		1910–1911	Nonparochial
George Rogers	Honorary canon	1900–1901	Rector, St. Luke's, Montclair
Dan Lewis	Residential canon	1901	Jarvis Hall
		1902	Wolfe Hall
C. I. Mills	Honorary canon	1909–1911	Rector, Ascension, Denver
B. W. Bonell	Honorary canon	1912–1915	Rector, Trinity, Greeley
T. C. Johnson	Honorary canon	1912	Rector, St. John's, Boulder
T. A. Schofield	Honorary canon	1912–1915	Archdeacon
G. H. Holoran	Residential canon	1913–1915	Rector, Trinity Memorial, Denver
C. H. Shutt	Honorary canon	1913–1915	Rector, St. Luke's, Fort Collins

The Vestries of Saint John's Church in the Wilderness

The charter of Saint John's Church in the Wilderness provided for ten vestry members including a senior warden and a junior warden. [The congregation elected ten vestry members; the wardens were then elected by the vestry.]

1860, JANUARY——A TEMPORARY VESTRY

Senior warden: Thomas J. Bayaud
Junior warden: Samuel L. Curtis
D. C. Collier
C. E. Cooley
Charles A. Lawrence
Dr. A. F. Peck
Amos Steck
E. Waterbury
Richard E. Whitsitt
Thomas G. Wildman

1860, EASTER——FIRST PARISH MEETING

Senior warden: Thomas J. Bayaud
Junior warden: Samuel L. Curtis
Henry J. Buckley[†]
O. P. Ingalls[†]
Charles A. Lawrence[†]
Dr. Drake McDowell[†]
Henry J. Rogers
Andrew Sagendorf[†]

Amos Steck
Thomas G. Wildman

[†]*replaced in December by: Dr. E. Arnold; James E. Dalliba; John S. Fillmore; R. A. Hunt; Roswell W. Roath*

1861, EASTER——ANNUAL MEETING

Senior warden: Thomas J. Bayaud
Junior warden: Samuel L. Curtis
B. H. Blanton[†]
Dr. O. D. Cass
Milton M. DeLano
John S. Fillmore
Roswell W. Roath
Henry J. Rogers
Amos Steck
Thomas G. Wildman

[†]*replaced in December by: Dr. J. H. Morrison*

1862, EASTER ANNUAL MEETING

Senior warden: Thomas J. Bayaud[†]
Junior warden: Samuel L. Curtis[†]
Dr. O. D. Cass

Milton M. DeLano
John S. Fillmore
Dr. J. H. Morrison
Roswell W. Roath†
Henry J. Rogers
Amos Steck
Thomas G. Wildman

†*replaced in June by: Senior warden: Chief Justice Benjamin F. Hall; Junior warden: Roswell W. Roath; Thomas J. Bayaud*

1863, EASTER—ANNUAL MEETING

Senior warden: Chief Justice Benjamin F. Hall†
Junior warden: Thomas J. Bayaud
James E. Dalliba†
Milton M. DeLano
Luther Kountz
Dr. J. H. Morrison
Dr. O. D. Munson†
William Porter
Roswell W. Roath
Amos Steck

†*replaced in September by: Senior warden: Dr. O. D. Munson; Dr. O. D. Cass; John S. Fillmore*

1864, EASTER—ANNUAL MEETING

Senior warden: Roswell W. Roath
Junior warden: John S. Fillmore
D. A. Butterfield
W. S. Cheeseman
Frederick Eckfeldt
John Dabney Grafton
Luther Kountz
Dr. J. H. Morrison
William Porter
Henry J. Rogers

1865, EASTER—ANNUAL MEETING

Senior warden: Roswell W. Roath
Junior warden: James N. Partridge
Charles D. Cobb
E. H. Collins
F. D. Hetrich
James C. Johnson
Luther Kountz
Dr. O. D. Munson
E. P. Parker†
Charles L. Williams

†*replaced in June by: Dr. O. D. Cass*

There are no minutes for vestry or annual meetings for the years 1866 to 1870. By 1871 only seven vestry members were elected. The wardens were elected by the vestry.

1871, FEBRUARY

Senior warden: unknown
Junior warden: unknown
John Armor
Dr. F. J. Bancroft
C. S. Ezster
Henry J. Rogers
Lewis W. Tappan

1871, EASTER—ANNUAL MEETING

Senior warden: John Armor
Junior warden: Charles B. Kountz
Dr. F. J. Bancroft
Charles D. Cobb
C. S. Ezster
Frank Palmer
Lewis W. Tappan

1872, EASTER—ANNUAL MEETING

Senior Warden: John Armor
Junior Warden: Charles B. Kountz
Dr. F. J. Bancroft
Charles D. Cobb
Birks Cornforth
Frank Palmer
Nathan O. Vosburg

1873, EASTER—ANNUAL MEETING

Senior warden: John Armor
Junior warden: Charles B. Kountz
William B. Berger
Charles D. Cobb
Birks Cornforth
Frank Palmer
Nathan O. Vosburg

1874, EASTER—ANNUAL MEETING

Senior warden: John Armor
Junior warden: Charles B. Kountz
William B. Berger
Charles D. Cobb
Birks Cornforth
Frank Palmer
Nathan O. Vosburg

1875, EASTER—ANNUAL MEETING

Senior warden: Nathan O. Vosburg
Junior warden: Charles B. Kountz
William B. Berger
Charles D. Cobb
Birks Cornforth
L. H. Eicholtz
T. B. Searight

1876, EASTER—ANNUAL MEETING

Senior warden: Charles B. Kountz
Junior warden: Nathan O. Vosburg
Birks Cornforth
L. H. Eicholtz
E. H. Hiller
Charles B. Patterson
Alfred Sayre

1877, EASTER—ANNUAL MEETING

Senior warden: Charles B. Kountz
Junior warden: Nathan O. Vosburg
Birks Cornforth
L. H. Eicholtz
E. H. Hiller
Charles B. Patterson
Alfred Sayer

1878, EASTER—ANNUAL MEETING

Senior warden: Judge Wilber F. Stone
Junior warden: E. H. Hiller
Charles D. Cobb
Charles B. Patterson
C. S. Roberts
Alfred Sayer
W. R. Thomas

1879, EASTER—ANNUAL MEETING

Senior warden: Judge Wilber F. Stone
Junior warden: William B. Berger
Charles D. Cobb
L. H. Eicholtz
T. Y. Lyster
Charles B. Patterson
Judge E. T. Wells

1880, EASTER——ANNUAL MEETING

Senior warden: Judge Wilber F. Stone
Junior warden: William B. Berger
Charles D. Cobb
Birks Cornforth
George W. Currier
W. B. Daniels
Judge E. T. Wells

1881, EASTER——ANNUAL MEETING

Senior warden: Judge Wilber F. Stone
Junior warden: William B. Berger
Charles D. Cobb
Birks Cornforth
George W. Currier
W. B. Daniels
Judge E. T. Wells

1882, EASTER——ANNUAL MEETING

Senior warden: Judge Wilber F. Stone
Junior warden: Dr. A. J. Russell
W. B. Daniels
L. H. Eicholtz
E. A. Peters
Charles A. Raymond
E. J. Swords

1883, EASTER——ANNUAL MEETING

Senior warden: Judge Wilber F. Stone
Junior warden: Dr. A. J. Russell
W. B. Daniels
L. H. Eicholtz
E. A. Peters
Charles A. Raymond
E. J. Swords

1884, EASTER——ANNUAL MEETING

Senior warden: Judge Wilber F. Stone
Junior warden: E. A. Peters
Judge Hiram P. Bennett
F. W. Crocker
George W. Currier
Charles A. Raymond
F. F. Struby

1885, EASTER——ANNUAL MEETING

Senior warden: Judge Hiram P. Bennett
Junior warden: George W. Currier
F. W. Crocker
J. Milner
D. Rubridge
F. F. Struby
D. S. Woods

1886, EASTER——ANNUAL MEETING

Senior warden: Judge Hiram P. Bennett
Junior warden: F. F. Struby
F. W. Crocker
Charles Hallwell
J. Milner
E. A. Peters
D. Rubridge

1887, EASTER——ANNUAL MEETING

Senior warden: F. W. Crocker
Junior warden: E. A. Peters
Charles Hallwell
J. Milner
D. Rubridge
J. M. Walker
Judge Youley

1888, EASTER—ANNUAL MEETING

Senior warden: E. A. Peters
Junior warden: Charles Hallwell
J. Baxter
F. L. Drake
Judge Moses Hallett
F. A. Keener
J. M. Walker

1889, EASTER—ANNUAL MEETING

Senior warden: Judge Moses Hallett
Junior warden: J. M. Walker
H. J. Aldrich
J. Baxter
Charles D. Cobb
F. L. Drake
F. A. Keener

1890, EASTER—ANNUAL MEETING

Senior warden: Judge Moses Hallett
Junior warden: Charles D. Cobb
H. J. Aldrich
J. Baxter
F. L. Drake
F. A. Keener
E. L. Raymond

1891, EASTER—ANNUAL MEETING

Senior warden: Charles D. Cobb
Junior warden: George J. Boal
H. J. Aldrich
W. H. Bryant
E. S. Kassler
G. Miller
E. L. Raymond

1892, EASTER—ANNUAL MEETING

Senior warden: George J. Boal
Junior warden: E. L. Raymond
H. J. Aldrich
W. H. Bryant
G. Miller
G. Niblock
W. H. Smiley

1893, EASTER—ANNUAL MEETING

Senior warden: George J. Boal
Junior warden: G. Miller
H. J. Aldrich
George Berger
W. H. Bryant
Alfred Rickards
W. H. Smiley

1894, EASTER—ANNUAL MEETING

Senior warden: William Ruth
Junior warden: Judge J. W. LeFevre
H. J. Aldrich
George Berger
W. H. Smiley
W. B. Tebbetts
H. G. White

1895, EASTER—ANNUAL MEETING

Senior warden: Judge J. W. LeFevre
Junior warden: W. B. Tebbetts
George Berger
John L. Stearns
Col. Thomas Ward
George Westlake
H. G. White

1896, EASTER—ANNUAL MEETING

Senior warden: Judge J. W. LeFevre
Junior warden: W. B. Tebbetts
George Berger
George B. Hooker
John L. Stearns
George Westlake
H. G. White

1897, EASTER—ANNUAL MEETING

Senior warden: George Westlake
Junior warden: George B. Hooker
John Best
George H. Knifton
S. F. Rathvon
Milo A. Smith
John L. Stearns

1898, EASTER—ANNUAL MEETING

Senior warden: John Best
Junior warden: S. F. Rathvon
H. P. Ellis
George H. Knifton
Harold Pearce
Milo A. Smith
John L. Stearns

1899, EASTER—ANNUAL MEETING

Senior warden: S. F. Rathvon
Junior warden: Milo A. Smith
Charles D. Cobb
H. P. Ellis
George H. Knifton
Harold Pearce
John L. Stearns

1900, EASTER—ANNUAL MEETING

Senior warden: S. F. Rathvon
Junior warden: Charles D. Cobb
H. P. Ellis
C. F. Hendrie
George H. Knifton
Harold Pearce
John L. Stearns

1901, EASTER—ANNUAL MEETING

Senior warden: S. F. Rathvon
Junior warden: Charles D. Cobb
E. LeNear Foster
William B. Harrison
George H. Knifton
Frederick W. Standart
John L Stearns

1902, EASTER—ANNUAL MEETING

Senior warden: S. F. Rathvon
Junior warden: Charles D. Cobb
E. LeNear Foster
William B. Harrison
George H. Knifton
Frederick W. Standart
John L. Stearns

1903, EASTER—ANNUAL MEETING

Senior warden: S. F. Rathvon
Junior warden: Charles D. Cobb
E. LeNear Foster
William B. Harrison
George H. Knifton
Frederick W. Standart
John L. Stearns

1904, EASTER——ANNUAL MEETING

Senior warden: S. F. Rathvon
Junior warden: Walter Fairbanks
D. Kinney
George H. Knifton
Henry F. May
John L. Stearns
Frank M. Taylor

1905, EASTER——ANNUAL MEETING

Senior warden: Walter Fairbanks
Junior warden: D. Kinney
George H. Knifton
Henry F. May
George Nash
John L. Stearns
Frank M. Taylor

1906, EASTER——ANNUAL MEETING

Senior warden: S. F. Rathvon
Junior warden: Charles D. Cobb
H. P. Ellis
Charles A. Johnson
George H. Knifton
Henry F. May
Frank M. Taylor

1907, EASTER——ANNUAL MEETING

Senior warden: S. F. Rathvon
Junior warden: Charles D. Cobb
Duncan Bond
H. P. Ellis
Charles A. Johnson
Henry Van Kleeck
Thomas Ward

1908, EASTER——ANNUAL MEETING

Senior warden: S. F. Rathvon
Junior warden: Charles D. Cobb
Duncan Bond
H. P. Ellis
Charles A. Johnson
Henry Van Kleeck
Thomas Ward

1909, EASTER——ANNUAL MEETING

Senior warden: Thomas Ward
Junior warden: Charles A. Johnson
William B. Berger
Duncan Bond
Clayton C. Dorsey
Harry James
Thomas S. Rattle

In 1910, the vestry was enlarged to ten members according to the provisions of the charter of 1861. For the first time, wardens were elected by the congregation.

1910, EASTER——ANNUAL MEETING

Senior warden: Charles A. Johnson
Junior warden: Thomas S. Rattle
William B. Berger
Clayton C. Dorsey
Frank Dillingham
Charles H. Hanington
Harry James
J. M. Maxwell
W. L. Pitcaithly
Judge Platt Rogers

1911, EASTER——ANNUAL MEETING

Senior warden: Charles A. Johnson
Junior warden: Thomas S. Rattle
William B. Berger
Clayton C. Dorsey
Frank Dillingham
Charles H. Hanington
Harry James
George H. Knifton
W. L. Pitcaithly
Judge Platt Rogers

1912, EASTER——ANNUAL MEETING

Senior warden: Charles A. Johnson
Junior warden: Thomas S. Rattle
F. M. Atterholt
Charles H. Hanington
Robert W. Hanington
George H. Knifton
Harold Kountz
James H. Pershing
W. L. Pitcaithly
Judge Platt Rogers

1913, EASTER——ANNUAL MEETING

Senior warden: Charles A. Johnson
Junior warden: Thomas S. Rattle
F. M. Atterholt
George B. Berger
Robert W. Hanington
George H. Knifton
Dr. L. E. Lemen
E. A. Peters
James H. Pershing
Ethelbert Ward

1914, EASTER——ANNUAL MEETING

Senior warden: Charles A. Johnson
Junior warden: Thomas S. Rattle
F. M. Atterholt
George B. Berger
Robert W. Hanington
Dr. L. E. Lemen
Frank L. Lord
James H. Pershing
E. A. Peters
Ethelbert Ward

1915——EASTER ANNUAL MEETING

Senior Warden: Charles A. Johnson
Junior Warden: Thomas S. Rattle
Charles L. Avery
Alfred B. Bell
George B. Berger
Lucius F. Hallett
Dr. L. E. Lemen
Frank J. Lord
E. A. Peters
Ethelbert Ward

1916, EASTER——ANNUAL MEETING

Senior warden: Charles A. Johnson
Junior warden: Thomas S. Rattle
Charles L. Avery
Alfred B. Bell
Henry H. Clark
Clayton C. Dorsey
Lucius F. Hallett
Frank J. Lord
Charles G. Mantz
Edward D. Upham

1917, EASTER—ANNUAL MEETING

Senior warden: Charles A. Johnson
Junior warden: Thomas S. Rattle
Alfred B. Bell
F. J. Chamberlin
Henry H. Clark
Clayton C. Dorsey
Theron R. Field
Lucius F. Hallett
Charles G. Mantz
Edward D. Upham

1918, EASTER—ANNUAL MEETING

Senior warden: Charles A. Johnson
Junior warden: Thomas S. Rattle
Harry Bellamy
George B. Berger
F. J. Chamberlin
Henry H. Clark
Clayton C. Dorsey
Theron R. Field
Lucius F. Hallett
Frank M. Taylor

In 1919, the annual meeting of the parish was
moved to January.

1919, JANUARY—ANNUAL MEETING

Senior warden: Charles A. Johnson
Junior warden: Thomas S. Rattle
Harry Bellamy
George B. Berger
F. J. Chamberlin
Henry H. Clark
Clayton C. Dorsey
Theron R. Field
Lucius F. Hallett
Frank M. Taylor

1920, JANUARY—ANNUAL MEETING

Senior warden: Charles A. Johnson
Junior warden: Thomas S. Rattle
Theron R. Field
William W. Grant Jr.
Lucius F. Hallett
Charles H. Hanington
Judge H. J. Hersey
Daniel A. Millett
Frank M. Taylor
Walter W. Winne

1921, JANUARY—ANNUAL MEETING

Senior warden: Thomas S. Rattle
Junior warden: Lucius F. Hallett
Theron R. Field
William W. Grant Jr.
Charles H. Hanington
Judge H. J. Hersey
Charles A. Johnson
Daniel A. Millett
Frank M. Taylor
Walter W. Winne

1922, JANUARY—ANNUAL MEETING

Senior warden: Thomas S. Rattle
Junior warden: Lucius F. Hallett
Theron R. Field
William W. Grant Jr.
Charles H. Hanington
Judge H. J. Hersey
Charles A. Johnson
Daniel A. Millett

Frank M. Taylor
Walter W. Winne

1923, JANUARY—ANNUAL MEETING

Senior warden: Charles H. Hanington
Junior warden: Theron R. Field
Harry E. Bellamy
Frederick J. Chamberlin
Clayton C. Dorsey
Patterson C. Fisher
Charles A. Johnson
Harold Kountze
Frederick W. Standart
Robert L. Stearns

1924, JANUARY—ANNUAL MEETING

Senior warden: Charles H. Hanington
Junior warden: Theron R. Field
Harry E. Bellamy
Frederick J. Chamberlin
Clayton C. Dorsey
Patterson C. Fisher
Charles A. Johnson
Harold Kountze
Frederick W. Standart
Robert L. Stearns

1925, JANUARY—ANNUAL MEETING

Senior warden: Charles H. Hanington
Junior warden: Theron R. Field
Harry E. Bellamy
Patterson C. Fisher
Charles A. Johnson
Harold Kountze
Frederick W. Standart
Robert L. Stearns

Dr. C. B. Van Zant
D. L. Webb

1926, JANUARY—ANNUAL MEETING

Senior warden: Charles H. Hanington
Junior warden: Theron R. Field
Patterson C. Fisher
R. H. Goddard
Charles A. Johnson
Harold Kountze
Robert L. Stearns
Frank M. Taylor
Dr. C. B. VanZant
D. L. Webb

1927, JANUARY—ANNUAL MEETING

Senior warden: Charles H. Hanington
Junior warden: Theron R. Field
R. H. Goddard
Dr. Henry J. Hersey
Charles A. Johnson
Harold Kountze
Frank M. Taylor
Dr. George R. Warner
D. L. Webb
Walter W. Winne

1928, JANUARY—ANNUAL MEETING

Senior warden: Charles H. Hanington
Junior warden: Theron R. Field
R. H. Goddard
Dr. Henry J. Hersey
Charles A. Johnson
Col. K. C. Masteller
Frederick W. Standart
Frank M. Taylor

Dr. George R. Warner
Walter W. Winne

1929, JANUARY—ANNUAL MEETING

Senior warden: Charles H. Hanington
Junior warden: Theron R. Field
Charles A. Johnson
Harold Kountze
Col K. C. Masteller
Daniel A. Millett
George A. Nash
Frederick W. Standart
Dr. George R. Warner
Walter W. Winne

1930, JANUARY—ANNUAL MEETING

Senior warden: Charles H. Hanington
Junior warden: Theron R. Field
Alfred B. Bell
Charles A. Johnson
Harold Kountze
Col. K. C. Masteller
Daniel A. Millett
Russell P. Raynolds
G. Frank Shelby
Frederick W. Standart

1931, JANUARY—ANNUAL MEETING

Senior warden: Charles H. Hannington
Junior warden: Theron R. Field
Alfred B. Bell
Charles A. Johnson
Harold Kountze
Col K.C. Masteller
Daniel A. Millett
Russell P. Raynolds

G. Frank Shelby
Frederick W. Standart[†]

[†]*replaced in April by: George Knifton*

1932, JANUARY—ANNUAL MEETING

Senior warden: Charles H. Hanington
Junior warden: Theron R. Field
Alfred B. Bell
Patterson C. Fisher
B. E. Gillis
Charles R. Hays
? Jackson
Harold Kountze
Daniel A. Millett
Russell P. Raynolds

1933, JANUARY—ANNUAL MEETING

Senior warden: Charles H. Hanington
Junior warden: Theron R. Field
George B. Berger
Paterson C. Fisher
B. E. Gillis
Charles R. Hays
? Jackson
Col K. C. Masteller
Dr. Henry VanHummell
Dr. George R. Warner

1934, JANUARY—ANNUAL MEETING

Senior warden: Charles H. Hanington
Junior warden: Theron R. Field
George B. Berger
B. E. Gillis
Charles R. Hays
Charles A. Johnson
Russell P. Raynolds
Robert L. Stearns

Dr. Henry VanHummell
Dr. George R. Warner

1935, JANUARY—ANNUAL MEETING

Senior warden: Charles H. Hanington
Junior warden: Theron R. Field
George B. Berger
Marmaduke B. Holt Jr.
Charles A. Johnson
Frank Lord
Russell P. Raynolds
Robert L. Stearns
Dr. Henry VanHummell
Dr. George R. Warner

1936, JANUARY—ANNUAL MEETING

Senior warden: Charles H. Hanington
Junior warden: Theron R. Field
Harry M. Hastings
Marmaduke B. Holt Jr.
Charles A. Johnson
Robert H. Joyce
Dr. Julius Kinney
Russell P. Raynolds
George P. Rider
L. R. Shallenberger

1937, JANUARY—ANNUAL MEETING

Senior warden: Charles H. Hanington
Junior warden: Theron R. Field
Charles F. Emery
Harry M. Hastings
Marmaduke B. Holt Jr.
Robert H. Joyce
Dr. Julius Kinney
George P. Rider

L. R. Shallenberger
Charles W. Webb

1938, JANUARY—ANNUAL MEETING

Senior warden: Charles H. Hanington
Junior warden: Theron R. Field
Charles F. Emery
Harry M. Hastings
Charles A. Johnson
Robert H. Joyce
Dr. Julius Kinney
George P. Rider
L. R. Shallenberger
Charles W. Webb

1939, JANUARY—ANNUAL MEETING

Senior warden: Charles H. Hanington
Junior warden: Theron R. Field
F. W. Carringer
Charles F. Emery
Winston S. Howard
Charles A. Johnson
Herbert S. Sands
Dr. Henry VanHummell
Dr. George R. Warner
Charles W. Webb

1940, JANUARY—ANNUAL MEETING

Senior warden: Charles H. Hanington
Junior warden: Theron R. Field
Harry E. Bellamy
F. W. Carringer
Marmaduke B. Holt Jr.
Winston S. Howard
Charles A. Johnson
Herbert S. Sands

Dr. Henry VanHummell
Dr. George R. Warner

1941, JANUARY—ANNUAL MEETING

Senior warden: Charles H. Hanington
Junior warden: Charles A. Johnson
Harry E. Bellamy
Dr. Alfred B. Blanchard
F. W. Carringer
Marmaduke B. Holt Jr.
Winston S. Howard
Russell P. Raynolds
George P. Rider
Herbert S. Sands

1942, JANUARY—ANNUAL MEETING

Senior warden: Charles H. Hanington
Junior warden: Charles A. Johnson
Harry E. Bellamy
Dr. Alfred B. Blanchard
T. C. Hitchings
Marmaduke B. Holt Jr.
Robert H. Joyce
Russell P. Raynolds
George P. Ryder
R. Ewing Stiffler

1943, JANUARY ANNUAL MEETING

Senior warden: Charles H. Hanington
Junior warden: Charles A. Johnson
Dr. Alfred B. Blanchard
Dr. Thomas Carmody
T. C. Hitchings
Winston S. Howard
Robert H. Joyce
Russell P. Raynolds
Herbert S. Sands
R. Ewing Stiffler

1944, JANUARY—ANNUAL MEETING

Senior warden: Charles H. Hanington
Junior warden: Charles A. Johnson
Dr. Thomas Carmody
T. C. Hitchings
Winston S. Howard[†]
Robert H. Joyce
Col. Allen S. Peck
Herbert S. Sands
R. Ewing Stiffler
Judge J. Foster Symes

[†] *replaced in April by: J. Melvin Moore*

1945, JANUARY—ANNUAL MEETING

Senior warden: Charles H. Hanington
Junior warden: Charles A. Johnson
Dr. Thomas Carmody
Dr. Gengenbach
Marmaduke B. Holt Jr.
Dr. Arnold Minnig
J. Melvin Moore
Col. Allen S. Peck
Judge J. Foster Symes
Dr. George R. Warner

1946, JANUARY—ANNUAL MEETING

Senior warden: Charles H. Hanington
Junior warden: Charles A. Johnson
Dr. Alfred B. Blanchard
T. C. Hitchings
Marmaduke B. Holt Jr.
M. Elliott Houston
Dr. Arnold Minnig
Col. Allen S. Peck
Judge J. Foster Symes
Dr. George R. Warner

1947, JANUARY ANNUAL MEETING

Senior warden: Charles H. Hanington
Junior warden: Charles A. Johnson
Dr. Alfred B. Blanchard
T. C. Hitchings
Marmaduke B. Holt Jr.
M. Elliott Houston
Winston S. Howard
Dr. Arnold Minnig
J. Melvin Moore
Dr. George R. Warner

1948, JANUARY—ANNUAL MEETING

Senior warden: Charles H. Hanington[†]
Junior Warden: Charles A. Johnson[††]
Dr. Karl Arndt
Dr. Alfred B. Blanchard
T. C. Hitchings
M. Elliott Houston
Winston S. Howard
Robert H. Joyce
J. Melvin Moore
E. P. Nieman

[†]*replaced in September by: Senior warden: Charles A. Johnson*
[††]*Junior warden became vacant*

1949, JANUARY—ANNUAL MEETING

Senior warden: Charles A. Johnson
Junior warden: T. C. Hitchings
Dr. Karl Arndt
Osborn G. Enholm
Marmaduke B. Holt Jr.
Winston S. Howard
Robert H. Joyce
J. Melvin Moore

E. P. Nieman
G. H. Roberts

1950, JANUARY—ANNUAL MEETING

Senior warden: Judge J. Foster Symes
Junior warden: Winston S. Howard
Dr. Karl Arndt
Walter C. Crew
Osborn G. Enholm
Marmaduke B. Holt Jr.
Robert H. Joyce
E. P. Nieman
Edward D. Pierson
G. H. Roberts

1951, JANUARY—ANNUAL MEETING

Senior warden: Judge J. Foster Symes
Junior warden: Winston S. Howard
Dr. Alfred B. Blanchard
Dr. Allen duPont Breck
Walter C. Crew
Osborn G. Enholm
Marmaduke B. Holt Jr.
Dr. Bradford Murphey
Edward D. Pierson
G. H. Roberts

1952, JANUARY—ANNUAL MEETING

Senior warden: Marmaduke B. Holt Jr.
Junior warden: Winston S. Howard
Dr. Alfred B. Blanchard
Dr. Allen duPont Breck
Walter C. Crew
Dr. Jacobs
W. Charles Kettle
Richard McAndrew

Dr. Bradford Murphey
Edward D. Pierson

1953, JANUARY——ANNUAL MEETING

Senior warden: Marmaduke B. Holt Jr.
Junior warden: Winston S. Howard
Ralph W. Becker
Dr. Alfred B. Blanchard
Dr. Allen duPont Breck
L. C. Fullenwider Jr.
Robert H. Joyce
W. Charles Kettle
Richard McAndrew
Dr. Bradford Murphey

1954, JANUARY——ANNUAL MEETING

Senior warden: Marmaduke B. Holt Jr.
Junior warden: Winston S. Howard
Ralph W. Becker
Roy E. Calloway
Walter C. Crew
L. C. Fullenwider Jr.
Robert H. Joyce
W. Charles Kettle
Richard McAndrew
Shepard Wright

1955, JANUARY——ANNUAL MEETING

Senior warden: Marmaduke B. Holt Jr.
Junior warden: Winston S. Howard
Ralph W. Becker
Roy E. Calloway
Walter C. Crew
L. C. Fullenwider Jr.
Robert H. Joyce
W. Charles Kettle

Richard McAndrew
Shepard Wright

1956, JANUARY——ANNUAL MEETING

Senior warden: Marmaduke B. Holt Jr.
Junior warden: Robert L. Stearns
Ralph W. Becker
George B. Berger
Roy E. Calloway
Walter C. Crew
L. C. Fullenwider Jr.
Robert H. Joyce
Dr. Oliver G. Stonington
Shepard Wright

1957, JANUARY——ANNUAL MEETING

Senior warden: Marmaduke B. Holt Jr.
Junior warden: Robert L. Stearns
George B. Berger
Roy E. Calloway
Walter C. Crew
Winston S. Howard
Donald G. McDade
P. R. Prangley
Oliver G. Stonington
Shepard Wright

1958, JANUARY——ANNUAL MEETING

Senior warden: Robert L. Stearns
Junior warden: Winston S. Howard
Watson A. Bowes Sr.
John Evans Jr.
John V. N. Hitch
Donald G. McDade
Gerald H. Phipps
P. R. Prangley

Dr. Oliver G. Stonington
Dr. Walter E. Vest Jr.

1959, JANUARY—ANNUAL MEETING

Senior warden: Robert L. Stearns
Junior warden: Winston S. Howard
Watson A. Bowes Sr.
John Evans Jr.
Marmaduke B. Holt Jr.
Donald G. McDade
Merrill M. McLaughlin
Gerald H. Phipps
P. R. Prangley
Dr. Walter E. Vest Jr.

1960, JANUARY—ANNUAL MEETING

Senior warden: Robert L. Stearns
Junior warden: Winston S. Howard
Dr. Karl Arndt
Ralph W. Becker
Watson A. Bowes Sr.
John Evans Jr.
Marmaduke B. Holt Jr.
Merrill M. McLaughlin
Gerald H. Phipps
Neil F. Roberts

1961, JANUARY—ANNUAL MEETING

Senior warden: Gerald H. Phipps
Junior warden: Walter C. Crew
Dr. Karl Arndt
Ralph W. Becker
Dr. Allen duPont Breck
Marmaduke B. Holt Jr.
Merrill M. McLaughlin
Dr. Bradford Murphey

Robert N. Murray
Neil F. Roberts

1962, JANUARY—ANNUAL MEETING

Senior warden: Gerald H. Phipps
Junior warden: Watson A. Bowes Sr.
Dr. Karl Arndt
Ralph W. Becker
Joseph L. Boettner
Dr. Allen duPont Breck
Dr. William D. Millett
Robert N. Murray
Neil F. Roberts
Dr. Oliver G. Stonington

1963, JANUARY—ANNUAL MEETING

Senior warden: Gerald H. Phipps
Junior warden: Watson A. Bowes Sr.
David M. Abbott
Joseph L. Boettner
Dr. Allen duPont Breck
Robert E. Jones
Dr. William D. Millett
Robert N. Murray
Burton A. Smead Jr.
Dr. Oliver G. Stonington

1964, JANUARY—ANNUAL MEETING

Senior warden: Dr. Karl Arndt
Junior warden: Watson A. Bowes Sr.
David M. Abbott
Joseph L. Boettner
Dr. L. Loring Brock
David V. Dunklee
Robert E. Jones
Dr. William D. Millett

Burton A. Smead Jr.
Dr. Oliver G. Stonington

1965, JANUARY—ANNUAL MEETING

Senior warden: Dr. Karl Arndt
Junior warden: Joseph L. Boettner
David M. Abbott
Dr. L. Loring Brock
David V. Dunklee
Robert E. Jones
Lawrence A. Long
Merrill M. McLaughlin
Burton A. Smead Jr.
John G. Welles

1966, JANUARY—ANNUAL MEETING

Senior warden: Dr. Karl Arndt
Junior warden: Joseph L. Boettner
Dr. L. Loring Brock
David V. Dunklee
Dr. Edward S. Johnson
Lawrence A. Long
Merrill M. McLaughlin
C. Wesley Schoelzel
John G. Welles
Robert I. Woodward

1967, JANUARY—ANNUAL MEETING

Senior warden: Joseph L. Boettner
Junior warden: Burton A. Smead Jr.
Dr. Edward S. Johnson
Lawrence A. Long
Donald G. McDade
Merrill M. McLaughlin
C. Wesley Schoelzel
Edgar A. Stansfield

John G. Welles
Robert I. Woodward

1968, JANUARY—ANNUAL MEETING

Senior warden: Joseph L. Boettner
Junior warden: Burton A. Smead Jr.
Elizabeth "Bill" Brown
Dr. Edward S. Johnson
Donald G. McDade
James D. McKevitt
Porter Nelson
C. Wesley Schoelzel
Edgar A. Stansfield
Robert I. Woodward

1969, JANUARY—ANNUAL MEETING

Senior warden: Joseph L. Boettner
Junior warden: Burton A. Smead Jr.
Vester C. Bradley Jr.
Elizabeth "Bill" Brown
James R. Burress
Robert H. Joyce
Donald G. McDade
James D. McKevitt
Porter Nelson
Edgar A. Stansfield

1970, JANUARY—ANNUAL MEETING

Senior warden: Watson A. Bowes Sr.
Junior warden: Robert E. Jones
Vester C. Bradley Jr.
Elizabeth "Bill" Brown
James R. Burress
Robert H. Joyce
Herbert S. McCall
James D. McKevitt

Porter Nelson
Richard P. Vosburgh

1971, JANUARY——ANNUAL MEETING

Senior warden: Watson A. Bowes Sr.
Junior warden: Robert E. Jones
Vester C. Bradley Jr.
James R. Burress
Richard M. Garrett
Robert H. Joyce
Herbert S. McCall
Mary McDade
Clyde Eaton Smith
Richard P. Vosburgh

1972, JANUARY——ANNUAL MEETING

Senior warden: Watson A. Bowes Sr.
Junior warden: Robert E. Jones
Lee C. Ashley
Wendall E. Beach
Marquis A. Bell
Richard M. Garrett
Mary McDade
Arthur J. Seifert
Clyde Eaton Smith
Richard P. Vosburgh

1973, JANUARY——ANNUAL MEETING

Senior warden: Burton A. Smead Jr.
Junior warden: William C. McClintock
Lee C. Ashley
Wendall E. Beach
Marquis A. Bell
Richard M. Garrett
Mary McDade
Arthur J. Seifert

Clyde Eaton Smith
Dr. Walter E. Vest

1974, JANUARY——ANNUAL MEETING

Senior warden: Burton A. Smead Jr.
Junior warden: William C. McClintock
Lee C. Ashley
Wendall E. Beach
Marquis A. Bell
Dr. Allen duPont Breck
Richard A. Kirk
Ivan E. Schooley
Arthur J. Seifert
Dr. Walter E. Vest

1975, JANUARY——ANNUAL MEETING

Senior warden: Burton A. Smead Jr.
Junior warden: Ernest R. Vetter
Dr. Allen duPont Breck
Robert Lee Druva
Dr. John A. Jacobey
Richard A. Kirk
Peggy Larson
Ivan E. Schooley
Dr. Walter E. Vest
Nancy J. Woodward

1976, JANUARY——ANNUAL MEETING

Senior warden: Robert E. Jones
Junior warden: Ernest R. Vetter
Dr. Allen duPont Breck
Dr. Watson A. Bowes Jr.
Dr. John A. Jacobey[†]
Richard A. Kirk
Peggy Larson
William C. McClintock

Ivan E. Schooley
Nancy J. Woodward
†*replaced in May by: Douglas R. McDonald*

1977, JANUARY—ANNUAL MEETING

Senior warden: Robert E. Jones
Junior warden: Ernest R. Vetter
Dr. Watson A. Bowes Jr.
Edward B. Cook
J. Clarke Houston III
Peggy Larson
William C. McClintock
Douglas R. McDonald
Arch L. Metzner†
Nancy J. Woodward
†*replaced in August by: Lura Williams*

1978, JANUARY—ANNUAL MEETING

Senior warden: Robert E. Jones
Junior warden: Douglas R. McDonald
Helen M. Arndt
Stanley P. Boehm
Dr. Watson A. Bowes Jr.
Edward B. Cook
Rowland O. Hawthorne III
J. Clarke Houston III
William C. McClintock
Lura Williams

1979, JANUARY—ANNUAL MEETING

Senior warden: David V. Dunklee
Junior warden: Douglas R. McDonald
Helen M. Arndt
Stanley P. Boehm
Edward B. Cook
Rowland O. Hawthorne III
J. Clarke Houston III

Mary B. Holt
Robert L. Poley
Lura Williams

1980, JANUARY—ANNUAL MEETING

Senior warden: David V. Dunklee
Junior warden: Douglas R. McDonald
Helen M. Arndt
Stanley P. Boehm
William Condit
Katherine Denious
Robert S. Gast
Rowland O. Hawthorne III
Mary B. Holt
Robert L. Poley

1981, JANUARY—ANNUAL MEETING

Senior warden: David V. Dunklee
Junior warden: Rowland O. Hawthorne III
Gladys B. Alexander
Dr. Watson A. Bowes Jr.
William Condit
Katherine Denious
Robert S. Gast
Mary B. Holt
Robert E. Jones
Robert L. Poley

1982, JANUARY—ANNUAL MEETING

Senior warden: Douglas R. McDonald
Junior warden: Rowland O. Hawthorne III
Gladys B. Alexander
Dr. Watson A. Bowes Jr.†
William Condit
Katherine Denious
Robert S. Gast
Robert E. Jones

Ruth M. Lanphier
Clayton D. Richman

†*replaced in August by: Rike D. Wooten*

1983, JANUARY—ANNUAL MEETING

Senior warden: Douglas R. McDonald†
Junior warden: Rowland O. Hawthorne III
Gladys B. Alexander
Dr. Robert C. Black
William H. Johnson
Robert E. Jones††
Ruth M. Lanphier
Clayton D. Richman
Joan M. Whitbeck
Rike D. Wooten

†*replaced in May by: Senior warden: Burton A. Smead Jr.*
††*replaced in February by: Susan H. Moore*

1984, JANUARY—ANNUAL MEETING

Senior warden: Rowland O. Hawthorne III
Junior warden: Richard A. Kirk
Dr. Robert C. Black
Mary B. East
William H. Johnson
Ruth M. Lanphier
Susan H. Moore
Clayton D. Richman
Joan M. Whitbeck
Rike D. Wooten

1985, JANUARY—ANNUAL MEETING

Senior warden: Rowland O. Hawthorne III
Junior Warden: Richard A. Kirk
Dr. Robert C. Black
Mollie P. Cook
Mary B. East
William H. Johnson

Richard T. Lyford Jr.
Susan H. Moore
Joan M. Whitbeck
Rike D. Wooten

1986, JANUARY—ANNUAL MEETING

Senior warden: Rowland O. Hawthorne III
Junior warden: Richard A. Kirk
Ethel Blantz
Mollie P. Cook
Mary B. East
John Lake
Richard T. Lyford Jr.
Susan H. Moore
Franklin P. Whitbeck
Rike D. Wooten

1987, JANUARY—ANNUAL MEETING

Senior warden: Rowland O. Hawthorne III
Junior warden: J. Clarke Houston III
A. Gordon Appell
Ethel Blantz
Mollie P. Cook
Dr. Gerald M. English
Virginia M. Erickson
John Lake
Richard T. Lyford Jr.
Franklin P. Whitbeck

1988, JANUARY—ANNUAL MEETING

Senior warden: Rowland O. Hawthorne III
Junior warden: J. Clarke Houston III
A. Gordon Appell
John S. Carter
Dr. Gerald M. English
Virginia M. Erickson
Joseph Paul Jonas III

John Lake
Charles L. Warren
Franklin P. Whitbeck

1989, JANUARY——ANNUAL MEETING

Senior warden: Rowland O. Hawthorne III
Junior warden: J. Clarke Houston III
A. Gordon Appell
John S. Carter†
Dr. Gerald M. English
Virginia M. Erickson
Mary Frances Johnson
Mary B. Holt Joyce
Charles L. Warren
Dr. William G. Winter Jr.

† *replaced in June by: Robert F. Buck*

1990, JANUARY——ANNUAL MEETING

Senior warden: J. Clarke Houston III
Junior warden: George P. Evans
Mitchell Benedict III
Robert F. Buck
Richard G. Fisher
Kathy Fleming
Mary Frances Johnson
Mary B. Holt Joyce
Charles L. Warren
Dr. William G. Winter Jr.

1991, JANUARY——ANNUAL MEETING

Senior warden: J. Clarke Houston III
Junior warden: George P. Evans
Mitchell Benedict III
Robert F. Buck
Richard G. Fisher
Kathy Fleming
Mary Frances Johnson

Mary B. Holt Joyce
Janet Q. Thompson
Dr. William G. Winter Jr.

1992, JANUARY——ANNUAL MEETING

Senior warden: J. Clarke Houston III
Junior warden: George P. Evans
Mitchell Benedict III
Robert F. Buck
Jack D. Finlaw Jr.
Richard G. Fisher
Kathy Fleming
Abigail Marsh
Janet Q. Thompson
Ursula Moore Works

In 1993, the number of members on the vestry was increased to twelve.

1993, JANUARY——ANNUAL MEETING

Senior warden: George P. Evans
Junior warden: Thomas F. Osborn
Robert F. Buck
Jack D. Finlaw Jr.
Nancy Hawthorne
Holly Hoxeng
Abigail Marsh
Will F. Nicholson III
Saundra L. Proctor
Merwin W. Smith
Janet Q. Thompson
Ursula Moore Works

In 1994, the number of members on the vestry was increased to fifteen.

1994, JANUARY——ANNUAL MEETING

Senior warden: George P. Evans
Junior warden: Thomas F. Osborn

Barbara A. Benedict
Jack D. Finlaw Jr.
Barbara J. Gillett
Rodger A. Hara
Nancy Hawthorne
Holly Hoxeng
Abigail Marsh
Will F. Nicholson III
Fred W. Pardee III
Saundra L. Proctor
Merwin W. Smith
Charles I. Thompson
Ursula Moore Works

In 1995, the number of members on the vestry
was increased to seventeen

1995, JANUARY——ANNUAL MEETING

Senior warden: George P. Evans
Junior warden: John Lake
Taylor S. Baird
Barbara A. Benedict
Lee Palmer Everding
Barbara J. Gillett
Rodger A. Hara
Nancy Hawthorne
Reginald S. Holmes
Holly Hoxeng
Thomas H. Keyse
Gregory A. Movesian
Will F. Nicholson III
Fred W. Pardee III
Saundra L. Proctor
Merwin W. Smith
Charles I. Thompson

1996, JANUARY——ANNUAL MEETING

Senior warden: Fred W. Pardee III
Junior warden: John Lake
Taylor S. Baird
Barbara A. Benedict
Kenneth R. Buckler
Virginia M. Erickson
Lee Palmer Everding
Barbara J. Gillett
Rodger A. Hara
Reginald S. Holmes
Thomas H. Keyse
Susan S. McKee
Gregory A. Movesian
Jay A. Swope
Charles I. Thompson
Robert A. Wagner
Lyn Zolman

1997, JANUARY——ANNUAL MEETING

Senior warden: Fred W. Pardee III
Junior warden: John Lake
Taylor S. Baird
Kenneth R. Buckler
Dr. Gerald M. English
Virginia M. Erickson
Lee Palmer Everding
Cory L. Fryer
Reginald S. Holmes
Thomas H. Keyse
Susan S. McKee
Gregory A. Movesian
William L. Strickland
Jay A. Swope
Robert A. Wagner

Emma J. Warren
Lyn Zolman

1998, JANUARY—ANNUAL MEETING

Senior warden: Fred W. Pardee III
Junior warden: Barbara A. Benedict
Kenneth R. Buckler
Dr. Gerald M. English
Virginia M. Erickson
Cory L. Fryer
Alice E. Knox
Dr. Robert E. McCurdy
Susan S. McKee
Scot Peterson
Virginia Schoelzel
Andrew D. Spinks
William L. Strickland
Jay A. Swope
Robert A. Wagner
Emma J. Warren
Lyn Zolman

1999, JANUARY—ANNUAL MEETING

Senior warden: Charles I. Thompson
Junior warden: Gregory Geissler
Dr. Gerald M. English
Cory L. Fryer
George S. Hoover
Alice E. Knox
Dr. Robert E. McCurdy

Scot Peterson
K. Marcy Pierson
Virginia Schoelzel
James J. Smith
Andrew D. Spinks
William L. Strickland
Jay A. Swope
Merle Troeger
Emma J. Warren
Lura Williams

2000, JANUARY—ANNUAL MEETING

Senior warden: Charles I. Thompson
Junior warden: Gregory Geissler
Dr. Bruce E. Bowler
Marsha Dawe
Gayle Ferrell
George S. Hoover
Alice E. Knox
Dr. Robert P. Lisensky
Dr. Robert E. McCurdy
Scot Peterson
K. Marcy Pierson
Virginia Schoelzel
James J. Smith
Andrew D. Spinks
David I. C. Thomson
Merle Troeger
Lura Williams

Notes

Note: for complete publication information on sources cited in notes, see Bibliography.

CHAPTER ONE

1. Letter to Bishop Whittingham from Kehler, December 1859. Maryland State Historical Society.

2. This house later became a school, then the site of the Windsor Hotel, and is now the site of the Sunset Park Apartments.

3. *Rocky Mountain News,* Jan. 18, 1860.

4. Record book of John H. Kehler, 1860–1868, 1871–1876, Colorado Historical Society, microfilm copy in Cathedral archives.

5. Hafen and Hafen (eds.), *Reports from Colorado,* p. 247.

6. The Episcopalians were second. The Auraria and Denver City Methodist Episcopal Mission, the forerunner of Trinity United Methodist Church, was organized on August 2, 1859.

7. Hafen and Hafen, p. 248.

8. Recorded by Dean Hart, *Parish Register,* Vol. I, p. 6, 1917.

9. Bishop Talbot's report, 1861, *Spirit of Missions,* Vol. XXVI, pp. 358–361, taken from Arps, "The Church Marks the Centennial," *Colorado Episcopalian,* January 1959.

10. John Chivington, the former presiding elder of the Denver Methodist district (1860–1861) is remembered for leading the Third Calvary against an unarmed camp of Cheyennes and Arapahoes in November 1864. The "Sand Creek massacre" resulted in the deaths of more than 120 men, women, and children.

11. Breck, *The Episcopal Church in Colorado,* p. 19.

12. Kehler also served as missionary to the Indians until, at age 80, he retired and moved to Washington, D.C., to be with his eldest daughter. He died there in February of 1879.

13. After serving in Bangor, Maine, and at Trinity Church, New York, Hitchings retired and returned to Denver about 1890. He lived at the Denver Club, downtown, and had a ranch somewhere southwest of Denver. He was named rector emeritus in 1910. Hitchings died in 1917 and is buried next to the east wall of the present cathedral. His legacy created the first endowment fund for St. John's Cathedral, with two tangible objects being the Celtic cross next to his grave and the bishop's chair in the chancel.

14. Record book of the Missionary Episcopate of Colorado, 1865–1914, p. 477, Diocesan archives, microfilm copy in cathedral archives. Sacajawea was the Indian guide for the Lewis and Clark expedition to the Northwest in 1804–1806.

15. Moore had briefly served as Bishop Randall's assistant seventeen months earlier.

16. Letter from Bishop Spalding, Erie, Pennsylvania, January 2, 1874, recorded in *Vestry Record Book*, 1871–1879, 1882–1899, p. 57; cathedral archives.

17. This building, now called Emmanuel Sherith Israel Chapel/Student Art Gallery, is a part of the Auraria Higher Education Complex.

CHAPTER TWO

18. From his scrapbook: "I had sixteen studies each day taking from early morning until somewhere near six and from supper to midnight as well. Thus, early in life, the no time for mirth or trifling here idea got a firm hold."

19. Hart, *Recollections and Reflections*, p. 81.

20. Ibid, p. 91. Hart later recounted: "I regret to say that I did shoot a buffalo, but there is no more what is understood by sport in that feat than in shooting a cow in a farmyard."

21. Ibid, p. 92.

22. *Rocky Mountain News*, December 21, 1872, in Hart's scrapbook: "In one hour he explained everything from the planetary system, its influence on the tides, vegetable and animal life of the sea, and ended with an explanation that the microscope revealed what made the Red Sea red."

23. Hart, *Recollections and Reflections*, p. 104.

24. Undated letter from the bishop of Rochester, recorded in *Vestry Record Book*, p. 139.

25. Houghton later accepted the call of St. Mark's parish in Denver in 1892 and served there for twenty-five years.

26. Letter from Charles Cobb, March 12, 1879; cathedral archives.

27. Hart, *Recollections and Reflections*, p. 107. He sailed home on the Britannic, where he became friendly with the captain, Edward Smith. One day, while they were near some ice, Hart asked Smith what his custom was in such water. The captain replied: "I go as fast as I can for by so doing I shorten the time of danger." He evidently held to his custom some thirty-two years later when he was the captain of the Titanic on her maiden voyage.

28. Now called the commemoration of St. Michael and All Angels, celebrated on September 29.

29. Hart, *Recollections and Reflections*, p. 108.

30. Ibid, p. 105.

31. Bishop Spalding was also responsible for the founding of St. Luke's Hospital in 1881. Spalding House, a convalescent center, established in 1965, was named for him. It was later renamed as Spalding Rehabilitation Center.

32. Hart, *Recollections and Reflections*, p. 105.

33. The rector of Saint John's Church in the Wilderness is elected by the vestry. By definition he is the priest who is in charge of the parish. The dean of St. John's Cathedral is appointed by the bishop. By definition he is the presiding dignitary of the cathedral. Because St. John's is both a parish and a cathedral, we have both a rector and a dean. Historically the rector is instituted first; and then the dean is installed. Generally, but not always, this is done at a single service.

34. The first cathedral was never finished.

35. Hart, *Recollections and Reflections*, p. 118.

36. This triangular site is now a parking lot.

37. From an unidentified newspaper clipping in Dean Hart's scrapbook.

38. Ibid.

39. The Mile High United Way Centennial Report, 1987, credits O'Ryan, Reed, Hart, and Friedman with founding the United Way movement. But their records indicate that

Friedman did not begin his work with the Charity Organization Society until 1889, and that Mrs. Frances Jacobs, of the Ladies' Relief Society, and a second Catholic priest, the Reverend P. F. Carr, also played roles in creating the new organization.

40. *New York Evening Post,* undated, probably January 24, 1893; Hart's scrapbook.

41. *Rocky Mountain News,* January 29, 1900; Hart's scrapbook.

42. Ibid.

43. Initially, Dean Hart called the clergy that he hired to help him his assistants (referred to in the appendix as assistants to the rector.) Later he called some, but not all, canons. By definition a canon may be a clergyman who is a member of the staff of a cathedral to assist the dean. This designation was probably first used to denote some special responsibilities for these assistants beyond their parochial duties. Both titles were used until 1957, after which all assistants have been called canons.

44. Cathedral Offertory (service) Register, 1902–1908; cathedral archives.

45. Hart, *Recollections and Reflections,* p. 192.

46. Stearns, *A Historical Sketch of St. John's Church in the Wilderness,* p. 9.

47. Temple Emanuel, later greatly enlarged, is now the Temple Events Center.

48. Notice from unknown newspaper, May 14, 1903; Hart's scrapbook.

49. Unidentified newspaper clipping, "Will Decide on Cathedral Site . . ."; Hart's scrapbook.

CHAPTER THREE

50. The second and third place designs both were submitted by Ralph Adams Cram of Boston, well-known master of the Gothic Revival style who redesigned the Cathedral of St. John the Divine in New York in 1911. In correspondence to the vestry, Cram argued that it should have chosen an architect rather than a specific design. The same year Cram entered a similar competition held by the Military Academy at West Point, where his design for their chapel was selected. This chapel appears similar to one of the designs submitted to St. John's.

51. By definition a "chapter house" is the house in which the canons of a cathedral meet, usually presided over by the dean. This was the appropriate title in 1904 because of the

Bishop and Chapter organization and the canons appointed by the bishop. However, this building was also used as the parish house, which by definition is a building other than the church proper where the educational and social work of a parish can be conducted. Where there is no church building as yet, the parish house may be used for divine worship, although it is not a consecrated building. This building retained the name of chapter house even though the chapter ceased to exist in 1915.

52. St. Mark's Church held this position for a few years.

53. Printed flyer: "A Statement," signed by Hart, Kountze, Rathbone, & Thatcher; Hart's scrapbook.

54. The architectural Master Plan first defined in September 1997 (a portion of which is under construction at this writing) set forth as one of its goals: "To plan the site in a way that will preserve the option of completing the cathedral."

55. The Roman Catholic Cathedral of the Immaculate Conception, completed in 1912, was designated one of the churches in the United States to be honored with the title of basilica in 1979.

56. Printed address given by W. W. Grant Jr. on September 29, 1929, from the pulpit of St. John's Cathedral. One of the spires of Immaculate Conception Cathedral was again struck by lightning on June 23, 1997.

57. *The Denver Post*, November 25, 1909; cathedral archives.

58. Hart, *Recollections and Reflections*, p. 194.

59. Ibid., p. 195.

60. Unidentified newspaper clipping; Hart's scrapbook.

61. From one of several letters from Frampton to Mr. Heath and to L. E. Chalmers, Esq. (apparently his agents in Founders Court, Lothbury). Collection also includes several letters from Chalmers to Dean Hart, September 1915 to January 1916.

62. A second inscription reads, "under unprecedented difficulties connected with transport carriage both of design and eventually the glass."

63. Letter on stationery of Kaiserhof Hotel, Denver, October 6, 1913; cathedral archives.

64. Unidentified newspaper clipping; Hart's scrapbook. The new car was a 1916 Briscoe.

65. Unidentified newspaper clipping; Hart's scrapbook.

66. *The Open Door*, January 1, 1937.

67. The deanery was at 1324 Clarkson Street, the site of our present parking lot.

68. Address by Winfred Douglas to Diocesan Convention on April 15, 1936.

CHAPTER FOUR

69. Wolfe Hall, the Episcopal girls' school across Clarkson Street, had closed its doors in 1913, and Miss Wolcott, the principal, opened her own school a few blocks east on 14th Avenue. In 1920, the beautiful Victorian building was torn down and the Denver Public Schools began building a new junior high school on the site across the street from the chapter house. The vestry became very concerned about the activities of the children who would attend this new school and considered building a wall around the cathedral property to be completed by the time the school would be finished. However, the question was tabled and the vestry never acted on it.

70. Printed sermon of Bishop Irving P. Johnson given on October 2, 1921, p. 8.

71. Vestry minutes, October 10, 1921; cathedral archives.

72. Vestry minutes, December 5, 1921; cathedral archives.

CHAPTER FIVE

73. Letter to Mrs. Field, April 25, 1924; cathedral archives.

74. There is no evidence of any family relationship between Bishop Ethelbert Talbot and Bishop Joseph Cruikshank Talbot.

75. Service leaflet, June 11, 1925; cathedral archives. See author's preface.

76. Dagwell's First Report to Parish, annual meeting, January 13, 1925, vestry minutes; cathedral archives.

77. Among Merrill Hoyt's other achievements is the Colorado National Bank building and among Burnam Hoyt's is the Red Rocks amphitheater. Burnam Hoyt's Denver career was interrupted in 1926 by a commission from John D. Rockefeller Jr. to design Riverside Church in New York City. It appears from the drawings that much of the work on the parish house was done by an associate, John Gray.

78. *Saint Martin's Chapel,* memorial booklet, December, 1927, p. 2.

79. Arnold Rönnebeck was the father of present St. John's member Ursula Moore Works. Family lore maintains that Ursula's brother, a baby at the time, modeled for the infant Jesus. It is also rumored that Rönnebeck carved six toes on one of the angels—a deliberate "mistake" so as not to offend God with the perfection of the piece.

80. *The Open Door,* December 8, 1968.

81. Although the conference center in Evergreen no longer belongs to the Episcopal Church, Don Pearson, present organist and choirmaster, is dean of the Evergreen Church Music Conference.

82. Now called the Scottish Rite Temple, located at 14th Avenue and Grant Street.

83. Plan of subjects for clerestory and aisle windows showing those installed 1935 through May 1, 1945; cathedral archives.

84. Dagwell was consecrated bishop of Oregon in March of 1936.

CHAPTER SIX

85. Letter from Paul Roberts to members of St. John's congregation, February 1936.

86. Dean Roberts suggested that a preacher should abide by three rules: one, have something to say; two, say it; three, when you get through, stop! His own discipline, he claimed, was his all-sharing wife, Marion, who has been known to say: "Dear, there were three places to stop in that sermon and you missed them all."

87. Katharine Brigham, Episcopal Times, November 1976.

88. At one time called the "House of Yesterday."

89. In this regard *Westword* called it "The Best Rummage Sale of Denver" in 1987.

90. Vine Deloria Sr. was the father of Vine Deloria Jr., the well-known author and member of the Editorial Review Board of the Colorado Historical Society. The Reverend Harold S. Jones replaced Deloria as missionary of the cathedral in 1951.

91. This author was recruited for the choir as a boy soprano in December 1944, from Skinner Junior High School in northwest Denver.

92. Letter from Fred H. Meunier to Dr. W. E. Vest (fwd to vestry), December 17, 1973.

93. Letter from Carolyn Bancroft to clerk of the vestry, September 7, 1952; cathedral archives.

94. Letter from Eleanor Hart Hanington to senior warden, January 18, 1953; cathedral archives.

95. The dean's report of the annual meeting in *The Open Door*, February 3, 1957.

96. Clipping, *Denver Post*, February 22, 1957; Roberts file; cathedral archives.

97. Clipping, *Denver Post*, April 1957; Roberts file; cathedral archives.

98. Allen Breck, *Paul Roberts Remembered*, March, 1984, p. 7.

99. Ibid., p. 5.

100. Wes French, *Rocky Mountain News*, March 16, 1984, unidentified admirer.

101. Ibid., Mayor Tom Currigan, 1965 award.

CHAPTER SEVEN

102. In addition to Nakata and Barrall, Dean Lea hired Bruce Ravenel, who left after less than three years, but returned to the cathedral in 1977, and Philip Gresham, who left in 1964 to join Dr. Lea in Chicago.

103. *The Open Door*, January 14, 1962.

104. Letter to Louisa Arps, March 7, 1969; cathedral archives.

CHAPTER EIGHT

105. Letter from Bishop Dagwell to Canon Barrall, June 28, 1962.

106. Reported in vestry minutes, June 20, 1963, printed in *The Open Door*, June 30, 1963.

107. The average attendance is the total of the four regular Sunday services, and does not include Christmas, Palm Sunday, Easter, or the Kirkin 'o' the Tartan. This high level of attendance lasted for four years, 1965–1968.

108. *Canyon Courier*, Evergreen, August 19, 1971, p. 12.

109. *Denver Post*, Glen Giffin, undated clipping, probably early 1972.

110. Wes French, *Rocky Mountain News,* September 24, 1968.

111. The *Proposed Book of Common Prayer* was approved at the 66th Triennial National Convention held in Denver September 8–20, 1979. This book is sometimes referred to as the "Denver Book."

112. For three years, 1975–1977, there was no 9:00 A.M. or 11:00 A.M. service, but only a 10:00 A.M. service. The low level of attendance lasted for six years, 1975–1980.

113. Letter from Barrall to congregation, December 26, 1979; cathedral archives.

114. Typed list and press release prepared by Olive Peabody for Dean Barrall, June 17, 1980; cathedral archives.

CHAPTER NINE

115. Barbara Benedict, *Colorado Episcopalian,* April 1981, p. 3.

116. Bishop's sermon reported by Salome Breck, *Colorado Episcopalian,* April 1981, p. 1.

117. Glen Giffin, *Denver Post,* February 21, 1982.

118. In addition to O'Neill and Morgan, McPhail hired Paul Robinson who stayed less than one year; James Frensley, who remained a little more than two years before returning to Texas; Kenneth Near, who served as canon and vicar of St. Andrew's mission; Richard Shackleford, who served three years; and Sarah Butler, who served as deacon for three years before being ordained a priest. O'Neill, Near, and Shackleford left St. John's shortly before Charles Kiblinger became dean.

119. Wes French, *Rocky Mountain News,* November 26, 1982.

120. St. John's Annual Report, 1982, ushers' report and personal recollections of head usher.

121. St. John's Annual Report, 1982, dean's report.

122. Terry Mattingly, *Rocky Mountain News,* October 20, 1986.

123. Ibid.

124. *Anglican Digest,* Michaelmas A.D. 1985, vol. 27, no. 5, pp. 4–9.

125. Photo copy of undated (1989) article by Elizabeth Eisenstadt from unidentified church publication.

126. Bishop Frey's sermon on January 14, 1990.

127. McPhail, "Out of the Depths," *The Living Church*, May 19, 1991, pp. 10–14.

CHAPTER 10

128. Questionnaire and interview with Dean Kiblinger by Jeanne Collins.

129. Questionnaire and interview with the Reverend Delzell by Jeanne Collins.

130. *The Open Door*, March 1993.

131. This author remembers that a similar suggestion for enlarging the vestry during the period 1966 to 1968 was tabled and forgotten.

132. Questionnaire and interview with Canon Randall by Jeanne Collins.

133. Questionnaire and interview with Canon Berlin by Jeanne Collins.

134. Barry Bowman, *The Open Door*, November 1996.

135. Ibid.

136. Questionnaire and interview with Canon Wilson by Jeanne Collins.

137. Ibid.

138. Pearson has also earned the title of "Ironman of St. John's" from the Denver *Rocky Mountain News* for his weightlifting activities. "Don Pearson, organist and choirmaster at St. John's Episcopal Cathedral, lifts 600 pounds, and his trainer thinks he can handle 100 more pounds." This may seem like an unusual activity for an adjunct faculty member at Iliff School of Theology and the dean of the Evergreen Church Music Conference, the oldest church music conference in the nation; however, Pearson has proven to be a man of many talents.

139. *The Open Door*, May 1995, and Denver BachFest 2000 program, Spring 2000.

140. Mark Wolff, "Spotlight," *Rocky Mountain News*, April 1, 1999.

141. *The Open Door*, August 1998.

142. John Hoskins, *The Open Door*, June 1998.

Bibliography

Anglican Digest, The. Eureka Springs, Arkansas: SPEAK (Society for Promoting and Encouraging the Arts and Knowledge of the Church), 1959 to date.

Arps, Louisa. "Father Kehler's Denver, 1860 to 1876." *The Denver Westerners 1973 Brand Book,* vol. 29, edited by Dr. Robert W. Mutchler, 2–55. Denver: The Westerners, 1974.

Arps, Louisa Ward. *Denver in Slices.* Denver: Sage Books, 1959.

——. "The Church Marks the Centennial." *Colorado Episcopalian* (January 1959–March 1961). Diocese of Colorado.

——, ed. "Dean Hart Pre-Views His Wilderness." *The Colorado Magazine,* vol. XXXVI, no. 1 (January 1959). Colorado Historical Society.

Black, Dr. Robert C., III. "Observation upon the 125th Anniversary of the Cathedral Parish of St. John's in the Wilderness, Denver, Colorado." January 27, 1985. 3-page unpublished typescript.

Breck, Allen D. "Episcopalians," in *Faith on the Frontier: Religion in Colorado before August 1876,* edited by Louisa Ward Arps, 48–55. Denver: Colorado Council of Churches, 1976.

——. *Paul Roberts Remembered.* Denver: St. Martha's Guild, 1984. 7 pp.

Breck, Allen duPont. *The Episcopal Church in Colorado 1860–1963.* Denver: Big Mountain Press, 1963.

Byrne, The Reverend Francis. Diary. Photocopy, cathedral archives.

Cobb, Charles D. Copy of letter to Rev. H. Martyn Hart, Denver, March 12, 1879. Cathedral archives.

Cathedral Chapter of the Brotherhood of St. Andrew. *Collection of Encouraging Thoughts Compiled from the Experiences of Great Men and Women.* Denver: The Cathedral Chapter of the Brotherhood of St. Andrew, Easter, 1903. 43 pp.

Church Pension Fund. *The Hymnal 1940 Companion.* Norwood, Mass.: The Plimpton Press, 1940; rev. 1951.

Commission of Architecture and the Allied Arts of the Diocese of Colorado. *Saint Martins [sic] Chapel.* Denver: Author, [1928].

Denver Post. 1896–2000.

Diocese of Colorado. Church newspapers: *The Western Churchman,* 1884–1887, 1899–1903; *Western Nuncio,* 1893–1895; *Colorado Churchman,* 1897–1899, 1906–1914, 1930–1931; *Our Church Paper,* 1932–1934; *Colorado Episcopalian,* 1941–2000.

——. *Clergy,* 1881–1923. Microfiche copy in cathedral archives.

——. *Journal of Annual Convocation,* 1887–2000. In diocesan archives.

Dorsett, Lyle W. *The Queen City: A History of Denver.* Boulder: Pruett Publishing Company, 1977.

Douglas, Winfred. *The Diocese of Colorado and Its First Bishop and Dean.* N.p., April 15, 1936.

Emmanuel Church, Denver. Record books, 1893–1908. Microfiche copies in cathedral archives.

Episcopal Church Annual. (Includes: The Churchman's Almanac, 1830–1881; *Living Church Annual,* 1992–1908; *Living Church Annual & Churchman's Almanac,* 1909–1931; *Living Church Annual,* 1932–1952; *Episcopal Church Annual,* 1953–2000). Current publisher: Harrrisburg, Penn.: Morehouse Publishing Company.

Episcopal Church Directory. (Includes: *Lloyd's Church Directory,* 1989–1911; *American Church Directory,* 1912–1916; *Stowe's Clerical Directory,* 1917–1925; *Episcopal Clergy Directory,* 1926–1972; *Episcopal Clerical Directory,* 1975–1999, biennial). Current publisher: New York: The Church Hymnal Corporation.

Hafen, LeRoy R., and Ann W. Hafen, eds. *Reports from Colorado: The Wildman Letters 1859–1865.* The Far West and the Rockies Historical Series, vol. 13. Glendale, Calif.: The Arthur H. Clark Company, 1961.

Hart, H. Martyn. *Cathedral Chimes. The Bells of the Denver Cathedral.* Denver: Williamson-Haffner Eng. Co., 1906.

——. *St. John's Cathedral Denver.* N.p., [ca. 1912]. 54 pp.

——. *Scrapbooks.* Two volumes. Cathedral archives.

——. Sermons, handwritten (approximately 100). Cathedral archives.

——. Sermons, printed (approximately 40), Denver: Alexander & Meyer, 1906–1919. Cathedral archives.

——. *The Organ.* Denver: St. John's Cathedral, 1920.

——. *The Ten Commandments—The Only Bulwark against the Avalanche of National Immorality.* N.p., [ca. 1902]. 10 pp.

Hart, Henry Martyn. *Priest-Craft, Roman and Other.* New York: Thomas Whittaker, 1889.

——. *Recollections and Reflections.* [Denver]: J. W. Hart, 1917.

Hornbein, Marjorie. *Temple Emanuel of Denver: A Centennial History.* Denver: A. B. Hirschfeld Press, 1974.

Johnson, Irving P. "Dean Hart—A Tribute to his Memory." Sermon by Bishop Johnson. Denver: Meyer Press, 1921.

—. "The Sermon." Preached at the Institution of the Rev. Duncan Hodge Browne, A.M., as dean of St. John's Cathedral and rector of Saint John's Church in the Wilderness. Denver, October 2, 1921. 11 pp. Photocopy, cathedral archives.

Kalvelage, David A. *Cathedrals of the Episcopal Church in the USA.* Cincinnati: Forward Movement Publications, 1993.

Kehler, The Rev. John H. "Record Book—1859–1875." Colorado State Historical Society Library. Microfiche copy and photocopy in cathedral archives.

Kirby, Linda K. *Heritage of Heroes: Trinity United Methodist Church 1859–1988.* Salt Lake City: Publishers Press, 1988.

Living Church, The. Milwaukee, Wisc.: Living Church Foundation, Inc., 1872–2000.

Missionary District of Colorado. *Journal of Annual Convocation, 1874–1886.* Diocesan archives.

Missionary Episcopate of Colorado. *Record Book, 1865–1914.* Microfiche copy, cathedral archives.

Noel, Thomas J. *Colorado Catholicism and The Archdiocese of Denver 1857–1989.* Denver: University Press of Colorado, 1989.

Noel, Thomas Jacob. *Growing through History with Colorado.* Denver: The Colorado National Banks, 1987.

Perkins, Mary Louise. *An House Not Made with Hands: A Century of the Episcopal Faith in Colorado Springs, Colorado 1872–1972.* Colorado Springs: Episcopal Centennial Committee, 1972.

Rainsford, George N. "Dean Henry Martyn Hart 1838–1920." Thesis, University of Denver, 1963.

Roberts, Paul. Sermon notes in cathedral archives.

Rocky Mountain News. 1859–2000.

Smiley, Jerome C. *History of Denver: With Outlines of the Earlier History of the Rocky Mountain Country.* 1901. Reprint, Denver: Old Americana Publishing Company, 1978.

St. John's Church in the Wilderness 1860–1927. Denver: Welch-Haffner Printing Co., 1927. 14 pp.

St. John's Church in the Wilderness. Parish registers (includes some historical information and parish lists), 1860–2000.

—. Service registers. Cathedral,) 1891–1896, 1902–2000; Chapel and in the community, 1927–2000.

—. Vestry minutes, 1860–1865, 1871–2000.

The Women of St. John's Cathedral. *Saint John's Cathedral.* Denver: The Women of St. John's Cathedral, 1979.

Saint John's Cathedral archives. Collections (including manuscripts, letters, articles, service leaflets, programs, minutes, scrapbooks, architectural drawings and photographs) by clergy, lay persons, organizations, events, memorials, and buildings.

Spalding, John Franklin. "The Cathedral and the Cathedral System." Sermon preached in Denver, January 11, 1880. Denver: Times Steam Printing and Blank Book Mfg., 1880.

Spalding, Sarah Griswold. Introduction and notes to "John F. Spalding, Bishop of Colorado 1874–1902," *The Colorado Magazine,* vol. XXII, March 1945, (autobiographical sketch) 50–57; May 1945 (letters), 129–140; July 1945 (letters), 179–185.

Spalding, William M., comp. *Outline of the Early History of the Episcopal Church in Denver.* Denver: N.p., [ca. 1933].

Spalding, William Marvin. *Personal Observations on Various Subjects.* Denver: N.p., February, 1939.

Spirit of Missions. New York: The National Council of the Domestic and Foreign Missionary Society, 1860–1887.

Stearns, Robert L. *A Historical Sketch of St. John's Church in the Wilderness.* Denver: N.p., December, 1927.

—. *One Hundred Years of Religion in Colorado.* Denver: N.p., February, 1959.

Trinity Memorial Church/St. Andrew's Church, Denver. Record books, 1887–1991. Microfiche copies in cathedral archives.

Witness, The. Chicago: Episcopal Church Publishing Co., 1917–2000.

Name Index

Subject Index

About Contributors to this Project

Everyone involved in the preparation and publication of this book has a history of engagement with St. John's Cathedral.

The author, Robert Woodward. Robert "Woody" Woodward's great grandfather brought the Woodward family to Denver in 1889. By the age of 3 months, Texas-born Woody had become a Coloradan, living in a one-room cabin with his parents on Willow Creek Pass near Granby. He graduated from North High School in 1949 and earned a Bachelor of Science degree in business from the University of Colorado, Boulder. While working as a professional square dancer at the Central City Opera House Association, Woody met, and in 1953, married Nancy Bell Joyce, the daughter of another pioneer Colorado family. Woody and Nancy spent their honeymoon dancing and managing a household of 17 ballet and square dancers in Central City.

As a 2nd lieutenant in the Army Corps of Engineers, Woody served in Kansas, Virginia, and with the Army of Occupation in Munich, Germany, where the first of Woody and Nancy's three sons was born. After returning to Denver, Woody's 32-year career with the Public Service Company of Colorado included designing the management responsibility accounting system used by the company for many years, and designing and implementing minority business programs as Socio-Economic Programs Manager. Retiring in 1986, his many civic responsibilities have included serving on the board of directors of the Urban League of Metro Denver.

Since singing in St. John's boy's choir in the 1940s, Woody has been a lay reader, chalice bearer, member and chairman of many cathedral committees, member of the vestry, and for 21 years, head usher. He's been a delegate to diocesan conventions, chairman of arrangements for the diocesan convention, and usher-in-charge for the Episcopal General Convention in 1979.

Woody and Nancy were appointed archivists of St. John's Cathedral in 1982, and they have been responsible for organizing, acquiring, and conserving the historical records that form the basis of this book. They completed coursework and workshops offered by the Society of Colorado Archivists, and a residency with the Archivists of Religious Institutions at the Friars of Atonement Archives in Graymoor New York.

Woody has been a member of the Society of American Archivists and secretary of the Society of Colorado Archivists. He has written more than a dozen articles on the history of St. John's Cathedral. His history of the 115-year old Deer Valley ranching corporation, of which he is president, is now in preparation.

Foreword by Dr. Allen duPont Breck. Dr. Breck, a lifelong communicant of St. John's Cathedral, was the official historian of the Diocese of Colorado and author of books on church history and the history of religion. He was professor and emeritus professor of history at the University of Denver from 1946 until his death in 2000. His foreword for this book was probably his last public word; he died a few weeks after completing it. Dr. Breck greatly loved St. John's Cathedral, and is missed by all who worked on this project.

Book designer Lee Ballentine. In 1960 Lee was asked by his kindergarten music teacher Estelle Parsons to sing in David Pew's 60-voice boy's choir at St. John's. He was confirmed in the cathedral with Mr. Pew as a sponsor. When Lee's voice changed, John Hancock invited him to become an acolyte, and from 1970 he was a regular acolyte and ran the sound system for the 7:30 A.M. Sunday service in the cathedral. At about the same time he put-on some of Denver's earliest laser lightshows at EYC dances in Dagwell Hall. In 1982 he was a pallbearer for John Hancock's funeral in the cathedral. In 1983 he and Jennifer Moore were married in St. Martin's Chapel by Canon Russell Nakata, where in 1993 their son Philip was baptized.

Editor Jennifer Moore Ballentine. In 1959, Jennifer was baptized in St. Martin's Chapel by Russell Nakata, where in 1953 her parents Ursula Rönnebeck and John Moore had been married by Dean Roberts. Her grandfather, artist Arnold Rönnebeck, carved the reredos in St. Martin's in 1928. Her father John Moore is buried in All Souls Walk and is commemorated in a garden walk and bench on the west lawn of the cathedral. Her mother Ursula was a member of the vestry and head of the art and architecture committee at St. John's in the 1980s. Jennifer met her future husband Lee in the parking lot of the cathedral.

Illustrator Betsy Johnson Welty. Betsy was baptized, confirmed, and married at St. John's Cathedral. She sang in the girl's choir under David Pew in the 1960s, and in the Cathedral Choir under Robert Finster in the 1970s and Donald Pearson in the 1980s. Her father, Edward S. Johnson, was a member of the vestry in the 1960s and a cathedral usher for many years. The cathedral's Casavant Continuo organ was given in his memory by Robert Woodward, Betsy's godmother Nancy Woodward, and Betsy's mother Helen Johnson, who was a founding member of St. Monica's Guild, Co-Chair of the St. John's Bazaar, and President of the Women of St. John's.

Publisher Gary Christy. Gary and his family first came to the Cathedral in 1960, and he taught 4th, 5th, and 6th grade Sunday School classes there in the 1960s. His wife Helen Christy has been the chair of the art and architecture committee, and as this book is being published, is a member of the cathedral vestry. Gary has been chair of the cathedral finance committee since the early 1990s. His press Prairie Publishing publishes books on the history and traditions of Colorado and the West.

Block 1 (1936–1946)

	1936 1937	1938 1939	1940 1941 1942 1943	1944 1945	1946
SAINT JOHN'S CHURCH IN THE WILDERNESS	Dagwell elected bishop of Oregon, Paul Roberts is dean, *The Open Door* published	Platt Rogers Kimball organ installed	Sunday school = 600, Membership = 1,750		
DIOCESE OF COLORADO		Bishop Fred Ingley			St. Paul's ⬤
CURRENT EVENTS		World War II begins	Pearl Harbor attacked, Denver census = 322,412	Germany surrenders, first atomic bomb, Japan surrenders	

Block 2 (1962–1972)

	1962 1963	1964 1965	1966 1967	1968 1969	1970 1971	1972
SAINT JOHN'S CHURCH IN THE WILDERNESS	Herbert M. Barrall, dean, parish house renovated		Columbarium built	Use of Trial Liturgy	Membership = 3,093	Choir win⟶ replaced
DIOCESE OF COLORADO				Bishop Edward B. Thayer		Bishop W⟶ C. Frey
CURRENT EVENTS	President Kennedy assassinated	Vietnam War begins		Rev. Martin Luther King Jr. is assassinated, integration of Denver schools, first man on the moon	Denver census = 514,678	

Block 3 (1988–1998)

	1988 1989	1990 1991	1992 1993	1994 1995	1996 1997	1998
SAINT JOHN'S CHURCH IN THE WILDERNESS	First Master Planning study	Charles E. Kiblinger is dean, Membership = 3,300			President Clinton visit	Master Pl⟶ program a⟶ *On This R*⟶ campaign
DIOCESE OF COLORADO		Bishop Jerry Winterrowd				
CURRENT EVENTS	Iron Curtain collapses	Soviet Union dismantled, Denver census = 506,000		Denver International Airport		